WAS ELIJAH A DISOBEDIENT PRIDEFUL PROPHET?

A Word From God Through Apostle Andy To The Joshua Generation

Written By
Apostle Andrew Giannelli

Charleston, South Carolina

Copyright@2016 by Andy Giannelli

Was Elijah a Disobedient Prideful Prophet?

A Word From God Through Apostle Andy to the Joshua Generation

ISBN #978-17322629-8-0

All rights reserved. This book is protected by the copyright laws of the United States of America. This book may not be copied or reprinted for personal gain or profit. The use of short quotations or occasional page copying for personal, or group study is permitted and encouraged. Permission will be granted upon request. Unless otherwise noted, all scriptures are from THE HOLY BIBLE, ENGLISH STANDARD VERSION®, Copyright© 2001 by Crossway, a publishing ministry of Good News Publishers. Used by permission. Scripture quotations marked (NRSV) are taken from the New Revised Standard Version Bible, copyright © 1989 the Division of Christian Education of the National Council of the Churches of Christ in the United States of America. Used by permission. Scripture quotations taken from the Amplified® Bible (AMP), Copyright © 2015 by The Lockman Foundation Used by permission. www.Lockman.org. Scripture quotations are from The Holy Bible, English Standard Version® (ESV®), copyright © 2001 by Crossway, a publishing ministry of Good News Publishers. Used by permission. All rights reserved. Scripture quotations are from the Revised Standard Version Bible, copyright © 1946, 1952 and 1971 the Division of Christian Education of the National Council of the Churches of Christ in the United

States of America. Used by permission. All rights reserved. Scripture quotations marked "ASV" are taken from the American Standard Version Bible (Public Domain). Strong's Concordance (Public Domain). Scripture quotations are from the King James Version. Copyright © 1982 Thomas Nelson Inc. by permission. All rights reserved. All rights reserved. Please note that this author and AG Productions publishing style capitalizes certain pronouns that refer to the Father, Son, and Holy Spirit.

AG Productions
Charleston, SC 29461
odm@homesc.com
Printed in the United States of America First Printing, 2021

This Book Belongs To

Date

───────────

Thank you for your support

PREFACE

When I minister, the Holy Spirit brings examples to help explain biblical truths. It may appear as if I am going down rabbit's trails but at the end it will bring clarity. I write the way I minister.

PRAYER:

⁹ And so, from the day we heard of it, we have not ceased to pray for you, asking that you may be filled with the knowledge of his will in all spiritual wisdom and understanding, ¹⁰ to lead a life worthy of the Lord, fully pleasing to him, bearing fruit in every good work and increasing in the knowledge of God. ¹¹ May you be strengthened with all power, according to his glorious might, for all endurance and patience with joy, ¹² giving thanks to the Father, who has qualified us[a] to share in the inheritance of the saints in light (Colossians 1:9-12).

Apostle Andy to the Saints of the Joshua generation who are also faithful to God.

Today there is an anointing spreading throughout the world. God wants the Joshua generation to avoid making the same mistakes that Elijah and others made. If we learn from the mistakes of these prominent biblical figures, we will not make the same mistakes. We will enter the fullness of what God has for this Joshua generation. We can also learn what they did correctly. (So, if we learn what they did correctly by fully obeying God and do that, and then also learn what they did incorrectly by not fully obeying God and do that correctly, we can completely fulfill what God has anointed us to accomplish for Him in this Joshua generation).

We will fulfill what Ephesians says in chapter 4: *[13]Attain to the unity of the faith and of the knowledge of the Son of God, to mature manhood,[a] to the measure of the stature of the fullness of Christ, [14] so that we may no longer be children, tossed to and fro by the waves and carried about by every wind of doctrine, by human cunning, by craftiness in deceitful schemes. ¹⁵ Rather, speaking the truth in love, we are to grow up in every way into him who is the head, into Christ, ¹⁶ from whom the whole body, joined and held together by every joint with which it is equipped, when each part is working properly, makes the body grow so that it builds itself up in love."* (Ephesians 4:13-16 ESV).

Many are saying how God is going to use this generation, including the children. I agree, but who is teaching or warning them how to stay humble and give God all the glory when He uses them?

This teaching came to me over 35 years ago, but God would not allow me to write a book on it. Every time I ministered this teaching, God added more revelation to the teaching. God told me on September 9, 2020 to write this book. The people God told me to ask for help with writing this book would not help. He said, "Wait." It is now July 18, 2021, and God is saying do it now.

Thirty-nine years ago, God spoke to me saying, He would use me to help bring the Joshua generation into what He has for them. I asked God, "Will I have to wait forty years like Joshua?" He never answered. It will be forty years January 2022.

Please take a moment before reading this book and ask God to show you which of the following places you are at right now on your spiritual journey. You are in one of these places: Cherith, Zarephath, Carmel, Beersheba, Horeb, or Cave.

The current Moses generation sees Elijah as a glorious hero because of the signs and wonders God worked through him. I am not sure if they have seen or talked about what God showed me when He told me to study the story of Elijah.

Jesus learned obedience from the things He suffered. (Hebrews 5:8) I asked God, "Was Jesus disobedient?" He showed me obedience is progressive. You do not expect a first grader to know or do what a 12th grader knows or can do. He showed me how He matured David, Job, and Isaiah. Moses and Elijah never received all God had for them because they did not wholly follow or obey God. They did not do everything God said to do or the way God said to do things. Abraham erred by listening to his wife and producing an Ishmael.

He even took Lot with him when God said leave your kindred behind. That action has negatively affected God's people to this very day. The reason Joshua and Caleb went into the promised land with the next generation was because they wholly followed God, not partially.

These examples are in the bible for us to learn from so that we do not make the same mistake of not wholly following God. We can walk as Jesus walked with the Father. Walking with the Father is saying only what the Father says to say, and it is doing only what we see the Father doing. It is being led by the Holy Spirit; no more or no less. Jesus said He glorified the Father by telling everyone what the Father told Him to say to them and doing what the Father said to do. Jesus said, *"I glorified You on earth, having accomplished the work which You gave me to do"* (John 17:4 ASV).

Back in the 80's, a minister on TV was talking about Elijah calling down fire. God said, "Study the story." As I studied this story in the Bible, I realized there were explicit instructions that said, "The word of the Lord came to Elijah" several times. Elijah went where the Lord said, but he did not fully obey what the Lord told him to do. There was times Elijah went and did some things, but the word of the Lord to him from God was missing. In those cases, Elijah was doing his own thing. Another example in Numbers 20, God told Moses to speak to the rock in the desert to bring forth water for Israel. Instead, he spoke to the people and said, must we give you water and out of frustration, he struck the rock. The thing here is the water came even though he did not obey God in just speaking to the rock.

There was a manifestation of a miracle through a man who disobeyed God's exact command. I realized signs and wonders do not confirm the man's obedience to God. The water came even though he was disobedient, which shows the manifestation of the water coming is because God wanted it to even though the man was in disobedience.

Here is the genuine tragedy, because he did not glorify God by obeying God, he and all the people spent forty years in the wilderness instead of receiving the promised land.

The word of God says, from the beginning there will be seed, time, and harvest, that is in the natural. God showed me in the story of Elijah that there are seasons in God growing us in the spiritual, just like in the natural.

When I was a baby Christian God showed me persecution and tribulation come on account of the word. They are like a tail on a kite which keeps you balanced. Without a tail, the kite flies everywhere with no control or balance. I will receive persecution because of this book. I ask you if you do not agree, do not draw a conclusion from your knowledge. Ask God if what I am writing is true or not. If you agree, ask Him if I am correct in what I am perceiving.

I ask God about Jesus being obedient. He gave me more insight twenty years later when my little boy was playing tee ball.

I heard His voice, and He said, "Is your boy playing baseball?"

I said, "Yes God."

He asked, "Does your son know baseball?"

I answered, "No, there is much more for him to learn."

Then God said, "When he is in high school, will he know baseball?"

I again replied, "No, there is more to learn."

God said, "When he is playing college ball, will he know baseball?"

I said, "No there will still be more to learn."

Scripture states *"Although he was a Son, he learned obedience through what he suffered;"* (Hebrews 5:8 ESV).

That's how God showed me we grow in obedience to Him. He expects it. That is why He expected Moses to obey. We can get to a place in God where we will not grow in our call if we are not obeying God where we are. We will not get to where He wants to take us in Him. We must be more obedient than what we are now. If you cannot be faithful to obey in little, you will not be faithful to obey in much. That goes for signs and wonders and flowing in the gifts of the Spirit. If we can learn by the experiences of the men in the Bible, we will not have to go through certain seasons of hardships. We also learn from personal experiences.

Jesus told the twelve, I have more to show you, but you can't bear it. What He was saying in our terms was, if I show you more, it will blow you away. He said, when I leave, the Comforter will come and all that the Father has is mine. I will reveal it to you by the Spirit. You do not need any man to teach you; but the Holy

Spirit, who the Father will send, will teach you all things, (John 14:26 paraphrased).

Matthew 16:21-23 ESV, gives an example of not being able to handle what Jesus was showing them. Jesus tells Peter something Peter could not handle.

²¹From that time, Jesus showed his disciples that he must go to Jerusalem and suffer many things from the elders and chief priests and scribes, and be killed, and on the third day, be raised. ²²And Peter took him and began to rebuke him, saying, "God forbid, Lord! This shall never happen to you." ²³But he turned and said to Peter, "Get behind me, Satan! You are a hindrance to me; for you are not on the side of God, but of men."

I believe this is where Jesus came to the knowledge that the disciples were not ready to receive the (more) He had to show them. That is why Jesus had to go so the comforter could do His job by taking them further into what the Father wanted them to receive. The Holy Spirit is a one-on-one teacher, and He will not teach you or try to teach you what you cannot handle. For whatever reason, you are not ready to receive what is next for you. In school these days, they send children to the next grade if they are ready to pass or not. That will not happen with the Holy Spirit. You will stay where you are until you learn what you need to know to progress.

When the Spirit led me to this story, I realized it was for me to be taught by Him. God wants me to share what He has taught me 35-plus years ago with you. Every time I read this story; the Spirit gives me more revelation or understanding on how to become more like Jesus, my brother, to only say and do what I am told and showed to say and do; that is the highest form of worship and praise.

I was on my way to minister in Africa and God spoke to me:

"I am tired of my people praising me."

I said to myself, "that cannot be God."

Then He said, "I want to praise them." Then I thought, I know that is not God.

He then asked me, "Andy, when your child says he loves you, how does it make you feel?"

I responded, "Good!"

God said, "When you tell your child what to do and he does it, you will tell him good job. I am proud of you. Which causes you more pleasure? Him praising you or when you are praising him?"

Then I understood. Just as He told Israel

coming out of Egypt, I am only asking one thing for you to obey My voice.

(Jeremiah 7:21-26) *Thus says the LORD of hosts, the God of Israel: "Add your burnt offerings to your sacrifices, and eat the flesh. ²²For in the day that I brought them out of the land of Egypt, I did not speak to your fathers or command them concerning burnt offerings and sacrifices. ²³But this command I gave them, 'Obey my voice, and I will be your God, and you shall be my people; and walk in all the way that I command you, that it may be well with you.'*

²⁴But they did not obey or incline their ear, but walked in their own counsels and the stubbornness of their evil hearts, and went backward and not forward. ²⁵From the day that your fathers came out of the land of Egypt to this day, I have persistently sent all my servants the prophets to them, day after day; ²⁶yet they did not listen to me, or incline their ear, but stiffened their neck. They did worse than their fathers.

He said "obey my voice" back then, how much more today should we obey His voice. The present-day Moses generation is doing exactly like they did back when they came out of Egypt.

God showed me a Christmas tree when I was very young in the Lord. Jesus was at the top of the tree. He said when I got born again, I was at the bottom of the tree. There were many of us. Then He said, the closer I came to being like Jesus, the less of us there will be. I told God the tree should be upside down, so there are more like Jesus. Ask God to show you where you are in the tree. To get to the top, it takes progressive obedience. I got born again in January 1982. Within days, God was talking to me. When He showed me the Christmas tree, I was riding down a four-lane highway. There were several cars following behind a loaded down dump truck. They were going below the speed limit. I wondered why those people did not pass that loaded down dump truck. God said, "They are like a lot of my people who are following an old loaded down pastor and cannot go any faster than him; but you will pass many of them."

There are seasons of spiritual growth. The three main seasons are: 1. separation from something to God, 2. refinement or being purged or pruned, and 3. fruitful field or plentiful place. God just showed me this morning that in the natural, the seasons all happen in one year. For the spirit man however, each season's length depends on the individual and how they yield themselves to the Holy Spirit and progress.

You will progress if you are willing and obedient. It also depends on you humbling yourself and yielding to God's instruction the way He wants it done, not your way.

Another example is in 1Kings:17-1 ESV, *"Now Elijah the Tishbite, of Tishbe in Gilead, said to Ahab, "As the Lord the God of Israel lives, before whom I stand, there shall be neither dew nor rain these years, except by my word."*

As you see in this verse, no rain manifested. But did it happen by what God told him to say or was it by Elijah's own words, like Moses leaving God out of the miracle of water coming from the rock? I perceive God told Elijah to say what He said, and the rain stopped because that is what God wanted to happen. Elijah said by his own word, not God's. I believe that is why God sent him to Cherith, because he needed some revelation of who he was not and who God was.

God needed Isaiah to see Him as Sovereign and then see himself as a man of unclean lips.

Elijah was full of himself. When you read the entire story, you will see this clearly. Do not become like this. Stay humble. If you had the miracle at your hand to perform, you should be like Jesus; only use it when God says to use it. Not at your will, but God's.

He who is faithful over little will be faithful over much. In the book of Matthew 25:14-30, there is a parable of the talents. The man with the ten talents was able to keep the ten talents. His boss gave him one more, because he made five more talents. It was not about the increase in wealth. His boss was looking for faithfulness because he needed someone to be over much. Are you being faithful to God or a leader of a denomination? Are you listening to God or someone or something else?

We have been bought and paid for and are not our own. When we get a paycheck, we can do whatever we want with it. We can obey

God's direct direction on what to do with what belongs to Him, which is all of it. We are not our own and all we have is His. So, the ministers say ten percent belongs to your church. That is one of the biggest lies that is being told from the pulpits today. No man's personal income was required to be tithed. The tithe was only on increase of items grown and increase of animals raised. No worker's income was required to be tithed. Do a study on where the tithe went in biblical days. Malachi 3:8 says, *will a man rob God?* He was talking about the priests, not you. Tithe was law. Jesus did away with the law. Once more, no personal income was to be tithed, just produce and animals. You have been lied to for years. My book on the tithe will be out by the first of next year.

God puts spiritual things in your hands to use for His glory. He gives you control although they belong to Him. You can use them as you want or as He directs you. You can do what you want or be led by Him, your choice. If you sew being led by the Spirit, you will reap by the Spirit, not by the flesh. Gravity works regardless of whether you know it or not; so, do God's laws. You can sew by the flesh and reap, but if it was not what God told you to do, do not expect to get His blessing on what you did. If you are His sheep, you will hear His voice. All you do should be by faith, which comes from hearing God, the Holy Spirit, or Jesus. If you say you know God and are not being directed by Him, you are sinning. If you are trying to live a spirit lead life, you are under grace. More grace than a child of God that hears God's voice and does things that God is not directing them to do.

God told me when I was born again, I needed to know what was being done with His money. I asked the people where I was giving my tithe and offerings, where the money was going that I was giving. They told me it was none of my business. As I was walking out of that church, God spoke to me. He said, "Andy, if you were giving your money to a company to invest, wouldn't you want to know where the money was being invested?" I said," Yes, of course." God said, "You need to know where my money is going." I was afraid of giving God's tithe and offerings to the wrong places. I opened a separate checking account to put the tithe in.

I put His tithe in that account every Friday. God would tell me what to give and where to give. That went along until one day God told me to give more than He had in His account. I told God He did not have that much in His account. He did not respond to me. That's when I realized all that I have belongs to Him. I need to do what He says, in other words, obey in all things with all I have control over, including my flesh.

I realized I was being told we were supposed to tithe, and that was not what God was saying but the ministers were saying that and if that was true, I believed it would be a slap in God's face. If we are under a better covenant, shouldn't we give Him more than those that were under the old covenant? That was 38 years ago. One of the easiest ways to hear from God is to ask Him where to give your money and how much? Many people are being told they need to tithe according to God's word, but it's not in God's word. They are giving it to churches and ministries that are misusing what they are told to give. It's not God. The ministers are misusing what belongs to God . You need to be led by the Spirit of God in your giving.

Many churches are saying the tithe belongs to the church. That is a lie also. The tithe under the law, belong to God. Tithe is law, and we are not under the law. If you are going to walk under the law, you need to fulfill all the law. We are supposed to be led by the Spirit in all things. Read the words to the song *What a friend we have in Jesus*.

What a friend we have in Jesus All our sins and griefs to bear. What a privilege to carry Everything to God in prayer.

Oh, what peace we often forfeit Oh, what needless pain we bear. All because we do not carry Everything to God in prayer.

Have we trials and temptations? Is there trouble anywhere? We should never be discouraged. Take it to the Lord in prayer.

Can we find a friend so faithful who will all our sorrows share? Jesus knows our every weakness. Take it to the Lord in prayer. Song by Joseph M. Scriven.

The first church I ministered in Columbia. It was for thirty days straight. The guy who took me there told the pastor God said to take all the pictures down of men all around the room. When I got in the pulpit, God told me to tell them they could keep up the picture of Martin Luther King if they put up Abraham Lincoln. The guy got back up and said God told him the same thing but he would not say it. That is what is going today. Ministers are not saying all God is saying to say. They fear man more than God. God told me years ago, when I am sent, I try to please the one who sent me. When invited, they try to please the one who invited them.

One day, I was teaching about being led by the Spirit in your giving in a church in Monte Christo, Dominican Republic. It was a little church with a tin roof and wood siding, and you could see right through from the inside of the building. This church, like many others there, did not have air conditioning. When I was there, God told me to give them my electric fan. Which I had to keep me cool in the churches with no air conditioning. That night I was in a much bigger church that even had air conditioning. When I got in the pulpit, God told me to do something I have never done before. God told me to take up an offering, match the amount, and give it to a young girl about twenty years old who had a baby. While they were taking up the offering, a young man came up and said he wanted to rededicate his life to God. He said he left his wife, wanted to get a job, and party, but nothing worked out for him. He repented and gave his life back to Jesus. Instead of praying for him myself, I had the pastor pray for him.

I called the girl up and gave her the money. She cried and wanted to say something. She was at the meeting that morning, and she heard the teaching about giving by being led by the spirit. When they took up the offering that morning, God told her to put two pesos in the offering. She said she told God she did not have any money. God told her to look in her purse. There were two pesos she knew she did not have before. She put them in the offering. When she left the church that morning, a lady walked up to her and gave her $10. God told her to go give the $10 to someone, and she told God, "I have no diapers for my baby." God told her to go give it anyway, so she went and gave the $10. That night she got $190. My interpreter said, "Andy, the guy who just gave his life back to God is her husband." For her obedience to God in giving two pesos, she went from two pesos to $190 plus her husband back in less the eight hours.

Quit giving God's money without being directed by God. What if God wanted you to help a widow, but you gave somewhere else? You buy what you want to buy, go where you want to go, watch what you want to watch, and so on. But you never ask God what you should do. One of the easiest ways to hear God is to ask where to give and how much to give. Try asking Him it works. He wants to bless your obedience and He will. Another easy way to hear God's voice is to ask God if you need to forgive anybody.

If you can't forgive them when God shows you who they are, just ask God to help you and He will. Unforgiveness binds you it does not affect the one you're not forgiving.

⁵Trust in the Lord with all your heart, and do not rely on your own insight. ⁶In all your ways acknowledge him, and he will make straight your paths (Proverbs 3:5-6 NRSV).

Religion that is pure and undefiled before God and the Father is this: to visit orphans and widows in their affliction, and to keep oneself unstained from the world (James 1:27 ESV).

When the Son of Man comes in his glory, and all the angels with him, then he will sit on his glorious throne. ³²Before him will be gathered all the nations, and he will separate them one from another as a shepherd separates the sheep from the goats, ³³and he will place the sheep at his right hand, but the goats at the left. ³⁴Then the King will say to those at his right hand, 'Come, O blessed of my Father, inherit the kingdom prepared for you from the foundation of the world; ³⁵for I was hungry, and you gave me food, I was thirsty and you gave me drink, I was a stranger and you welcomed me, ³⁶I was naked and you clothed me, I was sick and you visited me, I was in prison and you came to me.' ³⁷Then the righteous will answer him, 'Lord, when did we see thee hungry and feed thee, or thirsty and give thee drink? ³⁸And when did we see thee a stranger and welcome thee, or naked and clothe thee? ³⁹And when did we see thee sick or in prison and visit thee?' ⁴⁰And the King will answer them, 'Truly, I say to you, as you did it to one of the least of these my brethren, you did it to me (Matthew 25: 31-40 ESV).

When I read this as a baby Christian, I asked the Lord, "Weren't these Your sheep? Why did they not know they were supposed to do these things?" God spoke to me, "My ministers are not telling them." Why do you hear so much about tithing, church going, praising, and so on, but nothing about Matthew 25 and the sheep and goats? This is what God will judge you personally on when the Son of Man comes in His glory. This is a message to individual Christians. God is looking at YOU to do these things; not your church or ministry but you, personally. God does not say because you did not go to church, tithe, praise, sing, dance, read the Bible, and all the things you are hearing from the pulpit, "I will judge you." I dare you to ask God what you should put in the offering the next time you are in church. If God does not tell you what to give, then hold on to it. Maybe God wants you to help the brethren He sends you to after church. God says, *"My sheep hear my voice and another they will not follow"* (John 10:5 ESV).

If you are not hearing God's voice, focus on that first rather than what the preacher is telling you. Seek first the Kingdom of God. That means where God is ruler over your life and speaks to you to give you direction, instead of a church, denomination, or a man giving you direction. Teach your children as well. Do not expect a church to do it. God gave you the responsibility to raise up your children in the way they should go.

Proverbs 22:6 (paraphrase) says, raise your children up in the way they should go. Just taking them to church can hurt them more than help them. **You** raise them up. Are you reading the word with them? Praying with them? Serving and helping the needy with them? Are you feeding a widow and so on?

Children learn by your example more than going to church. The reality is, if you cannot do what the word says, how can the Spirit lead you? Why was Elijah sent by God to the widow at Zarephath, a Gentile, not a Jewish widow?

Ask God every day what you should do, even if it is a Sunday. God may have you visit someone who cannot come to church, like a widow or whoever. Rather than spending time in church. Spend time with Him. Over 35 years ago, when I read Matthew 25, it made me think of when Jesus said, I have meat (food) to eat you know not of. My meat (food) is to do the will of the Father (John 4:34 paraphrased). When He made that statement, He was at a well talking to a Samaritan woman which was strictly against what the Jews did. He said He was doing the will of His father, and she went running back to town to tell everybody about Him. Many believed because of what she said. Then they came out, listened to Him, and said, "Now we believe because of what He said."

Are you eating His food? I was just reminded by the Spirit, Jesus said to the Father, "If thy will lift this cup but none the less your will be done not mine" (Luke 22:42 paraphrased). Do you have a cup given by God for you to drink? If not, then you are not crucified with Christ.

When Jesus spoke of these things, it was in His third year of ministry. All but twelve of the disciples left Him. This is like most churches today that want entertainment, signs, and wonders, but will not allow God in the building to do what He wants. If you never need correction or direction from God, that means you are not doing anything for Him. The devil will bless you. Most teach that prosperity [money, finances] and all that goes with it, are from God. That means everyone who has a lot of money is being blessed by God; I don't think so.

Study the word "prosper" in the Bible instead of having the ministers tell you it is money and things. Did Jesus prosper like the ministers are telling you to? Was His prospering based on achieving what God called and anointed Him to do? The word prosper in the New Testament meant to accomplish, while on your journey, what you were sent or going to do. What does your minister, if you have one, have you focused on?

Greek word *euodoo* (G2137) means: "to grant a prosperous and expeditious journey, to lead by a direct and easy way, to grant a successful issue, to cause to prosper"

3 John:2 says: *"Beloved, I pray that all may go well with you and that you may be in health; I know that it is well with your soul" (RSV).*

Beloved, I wish above all things that thou mayest prosper and be in health, even as thy soul prospereth (KJV).

Beloved, I pray that in every way you may succeed and prosper and be in good health [physically], just as [I know] your soul prospers [spiritually] (AMP).

Dear friend, I am praying that all is well with you and that your body is as healthy as I know your soul is (NLT)

You can see it is not talking about money like you have been told over and over. It is mostly talking to Christians to accomplish their assignment from God in this world or what they're anointed to achieve God's purpose through them for the Kingdom. Prosper is a word you hear frequently mentioned in sermons, books, and other teachings.

In order to properly understand why God wants you to prosper, it's important to first gain a scriptural insight on what the word prosper actually means as defined in the Bible.

According to Strong's Concordance, there are three primary Hebrew words used to prosper in the Old Testament. H6743 is used 49 times, and it is translated as: "to advance, prosper, make progress, succeed, be profitable, to make prosperous"

2 Chronicles 26:5 says: *"And he sought God in the days of Zechariah, who had understanding in the visions of God: and as long as he sought the LORD, God made him to prosper."*

H7919 is used 8 times, and it is translated as: "to be prudent, be circumspect, wisely understand, prosper"

Deuteronomy 29:9 says: *"Keep therefore the words of this covenant, and do them, that ye may prosper in all that ye do."*

H7951 is used 3 times, and it means: "to be at rest, prosper, be at ease"

Psalm 122:6 says: *"Pray for the peace of Jerusalem: they shall prosper that love thee."*

There are two other words used for the word prosper (H7961 and H3787) but they are only used one time each. In Strong's Concordance, they are defined as: "quiet, at ease, prosperous" and "to succeed, please, be suitable, be proper, be advantageous, be right and prosper"

Interestingly enough, according to Strong's Concordance, the word prosper only appears in the New Testament four times in three verses. It's the Greek word G2137, which means: "to grant a prosperous and expeditious journey, to lead by a direct and easy way, to grant a successful issue, to cause to prosper"

3 John 2 KJV says: *"Beloved, I wish above all things that thou mayest prosper and be in health, even as thy soul prospereth."*

I want to share a recent story with you about an orphanage in Haiti called New Life Children's Home. Since 1977, Miriam Frederick has run this orphanage. During Christmas 2019, she hosted seven hundred children. She was shooting for 1,000 for Christmas 2020. In the summer of 2020, the Lord told me to ask her if she would like some tennis balls for the children for Christmas. She said, "Yes." God told me to send the tennis balls right away. I told her to give them to the children, and if God told us, we do something else for Christmas. She thanked me and told me the children had nothing to play with. There is not enough in the budget to get them anything. She said her diaper bill is $33,000 a year. She has older children in diapers as well as infants and young children. Because of her donors, she would have little gifts for the children at Christmas time. She helps many other Haitian orphanages.

I sent out some emails to some friends, the one thousand tennis balls were paid for and shipped to Florida where they will fill a container and eventually ship to Haiti. She told me about other needs of the orphanage. The next night around 10:00 pm, God dealt with me about sending more items. I went on-line and ordered 100 soccer balls with 100 air pumps, toy dolls, cars, beach balls, balloons, spoons, forks, dishes, cups, blenders, which they had none and needed to blend food for some of the children and more. Then, God spoke to my daughter, one of my nine children living at home, to send her some soap. She sent 130 bars of soap. Miriam was overwhelmed. We had family fellowship a few nights later. God spoke to me and said, "Remember what I did for Rahab, the harlot, in Jericho because she hid the spies? I am going to do the same for your family because you have obeyed me by helping the orphanage." You see its not always about money like some teach.

Miriam is a wonderful person, faithfully dedicated to the work God has called her to. If the Lord prompts you to help her ministry in any way, please do so. She has been in ministry at the orphanage since 1977. You may contact her at the following addresses:

World Harvest Missions/New Life Children's Home

PO Box 6462

Lake Worth, Fl 33466

Phone 561-868-5005

Email newlife4kids@gmail.com

Website www.newlife4kids.org

God just impressed on me to tell you of an incident I had as a young Christian. When I got born again, I could not put the bible down for three and half years. Every Saturday, I would fix my breakfast and read the bible all day. I got involved in prison ministry early in my walk with God. I went to see Ernie Torres about doing some accounting work for me. When he found out I was ministering in prison, he asked me to join them in the Kairos prison ministry. This was in 1982. I accepted the Lord in January of 1982.

Every Saturday, I would spend the whole day reading my Bible, just me and God. After joining Kairos. I ended up being busy with prison ministry for nine Saturdays in a row. On the next Saturday, I had nothing to do. I said to myself, "It is God and me today". I ate my breakfast and sat down to read, and the phone rang. On the phone was Anthony, a little boy I had met at a mission in North Charleston. He explained to me that his mother's mom had died in Virginia, and they spent their last $50 on fuel going to the funeral. Their car broke down and they were broke. He asked if I could help them. I almost said, not today, but I could not say it.

I went to their house and told them, "Come on, I will take you to get lunch." I looked in the refrigerator. It was empty; so were the cabinets. There was no food at all. It was February, and the house was cold. I ask his mother why was it so cold? She informed me it took $160 dollars to fill the oil tank, but $160 was all she made every two weeks. I took her, her daughter, and son to get something to eat. Afterwards, I took them to my house. We fellowshipped and ate supper. I had $850 cash that I gave them, along with a check for $850. I also loaned them one of my cars. When they left, I sat down, got my bible, and told God, "I am sorry, I really wanted to spend the day with you." I was very sad, but God spoke to me and said, "You did spend the day with me." That's when I realized who He is; the least of these.

Whatever you do unto the least of these my brethren, you do unto me (Matthew 25:40 paraphrased)

This is not being taught in most churches. I could have praised God all day that Saturday, but would He have been pleased? When I spend my time praising Him but not helping Him or doing what He wants me to do, do you think that pleases Him? If I had given that $1,700 to the church instead of that family, do you think He would have been pleased?

Many churches are taking the money God wants to go towards helping God {the least of these my brethren}. Spending it on themselves. They will not get a reward from God, but the opposite. I could say much more. I ask that you pray for yourself and ask God whether the church you are attending is where He wants you to be. Is your reason for going there by the direction of God or for another reason?

I was ministering in Columbia, SC. There was a lady in the prayer line. God showed me Jesus appeared to her outside her church and told her they would not let Him in the church. When I told her this, she said, "That is true. How did you know that?" I said, "God wants me to ask you a question, why are you still going there?" She never answered. I ran across her a year later, and told her, "God said you're still going to that church and giving His money to it." She said, "I like the choir."

This is like a lot of Christians who get married to who they want; not who God wants them to. Some fleshly pastors say, "Whatever God joins together let no man put asunder." God had nothing to do with it. It is not a marriage ordained by God. They should ask God is this really His will for this couple to be married, and if God says no, they shouldn't marry them. This happens every week.

You left the church God told you to go to. Did God tell you to leave? Well, you could say, "I was not getting fed there." Perhaps you were there to feed, not be fed. He used ravens to feed Elijah. Why could God not use you even to speak to the ministers? Most people are told to come to church to receive or get. Except, they are encouraged to give their money. You should not go anyplace with the mind to get, but to give the seed God has put in you to give. It is better to give than receive. That is not what is being taught to most church goers. They are told to come to get.

It is better to give than receive. Do not go anywhere just to receive; but go to give. Jesus gives seed to the Sower. You have seed everywhere you go. Sow it where He shows you to sow. God gives seed to the Sower. If you are not a Sower, you do not get seed. Think about that.

Maybe that's why you are not getting seed or the word, because you're being taught to receive. If you're not sowing the seed He gives you, you're not a Sower. That might be why you're not getting any word from God anymore, because you aren't sowing what He gave you to sow.

The true word of God does not convict most church goers today; but offends them. A good example is when Jesus said you must eat of my flesh and drink of my blood, all the people left except the twelve. That is why most ministers are manipulators and do not say what God would have them say and do. God told me most churches are synagogues. The synagogues allowed Jesus to do very little in their services. In biblical days, they ran Him out. The same with most churches today. If they let Him do anything, it is very little.

I was invited to a church shut in. It was 1982, my first year with the Lord. I told the person who took me there to call a person up for me to pray for. I prophesied their call, and they ended up having two churches.

I was in a service with them in 2019. When they closed the service, they told me God was not done that night, but they could close the service if they wanted to, even if God was not done. They died that year, much younger than me. I can tell you more stories of people who have died that I warned who told lies or would not obey God. I am not talking about baby Christians. One was a great man of God. God told him not to get on a plane. He did and he and his wife died in a plane crash on that same plane.

Then he will say to those at his left hand: *"Depart from me, you cursed, into the eternal fire prepared for the devil and his angels; [42]for I was hungry, and you gave me no food, I was thirsty and you gave me no drink, [43]I was a stranger and you did not welcome me, naked and you did not clothe me, sick and in prison and you did not visit me.' [44]Then they also will answer, 'Lord, when did we see thee hungry or thirsty or a stranger or naked or sick or in prison, and did not minister to thee?' [45]Then he will answer them, 'Truly, I say to you, as you did it not to one of the least of these, you did it not to me.' [46]And they will go away into eternal punishment, but the righteous into eternal life"* (Matthew 25:41-46 ESV).

The word of the Lord told Elijah to go down to the brook Cherith east of the Jordan. There, God would send ravens to feed him meat and bread twice a day. Notice it says *the word of the Lord came to him*. Can you see what God is trying to show Elijah? He is using dirty birds to feed him twice a day, probably for a year. God will sometime choose the despised things of this world to confound the mighty. He will use the foolish to bring the strong down to nothing.

I perceive Elijah never understood that God has him all alone and not using him. He is using the birds to feed him instead. God is working a miracle of provision through dirty birds. He is showing Elijah He can do anything He wants through anybody or anything, even a rock. God is trying to show Elijah he is not all that he thinks he is simply because He uses him. God used the ass to speak to Balaam and provided water from a rock.

He's not feeding himself. As a side note, if you are not where you should be, you will not get what God has for you. If Elijah was not obedient and was not in the place where God told him to be. I believe the ravens would have shown up anyway because they obeyed God. Maybe someone else would have gotten that meal.

DR. CL Oliver has written a book entitled En Punto, which talks about this. It is excellent! Also, Sons of Zadok. These books will be a spiritual blessing to you. His website is: https://zadokpublications.com/products.htm.

13And these ye shall have in abomination among the birds; they shall not be eaten, they are an abomination: the [a]eagle, and the gier-eagle, and the ospray, 14and the kite, and the falcon after its kind, 15every raven after its kind, (Leviticus 11:13-15 ASV).

How could God have handled the kingdom without Elijah for three years? I would perceive he would have been on the shelf or sitting on the bench. He would not have been in the field and taking part in what God was doing. I do not think he realized God was using an unclean bird (raven) to feed him. God said the raven was one of the unclean birds they could not eat. These unclean birds are feeding him good stuff they could have eaten themselves. As God feeds the ravens, he is feeding Elijah. Someone made that bread and cooked that meat. Maybe you're asking yourself, "Why is God not using me? Why am I all alone? How can God's world go on without me?"

Jordan means go downward or decent. Cherith means separation from something to God. Elijah understood what the names of these places meant. Did he realize what God was saying to him or showing him? If you are at Cherith, listen to God, ask him to show you what He wants you to learn. Each season's length depends on the individual. You can get a lot of sun [word] but not much rain [spirit].

Many today go with the word only. Jesus was the word, but only did what the Father said to say and do. He did nothing on His own and Jesus was the word. How about you?

(1 Kings 17:8-9 ESV) *⁸Then the word of the Lord came to him,*

This is the second time the word of the Lord came.

⁹"Arise, go to Zar'ephath, which belongs to Sidon, and dwell there. Behold, I have commanded a widow there to feed you."

Zarephath means refinement or purge away. We can say prune, to clear something totally out or away from something. Again, Elijah knows the meaning of the words of the places God is sending him, but is he paying attention?

God is going to work a miracle through a widow in Sidon which is an area of the Gentiles. The Jews despised these people, for they were not a part of Israel. Tyre and Sidon where Gentile regions most Jews would have considered unclean. The region in which these cities were located had a long history of paganism and opposition to the Jews. For instance, the wicked queen Jezebel was the daughter of the Sidonian king. She incited Ahab to worship the false god Baal.

She persecuted Elijah the prophet. God is sending Elijah to a Gentile widow, not a Jew, to work a miracle through her for him. I have to say again, God is trying to get his attention off himself. Working a miracle through a Gentile woman so He could be sustained. God is showing him he can use a gentile for His purpose. Same as God is using Elijah for His purpose; or a rock, or a bird or an ass or you or me, etc.

(1 Kings 17:10-16 ESV) *"So he arose and went to Zar'ephath; and when he came to the gate of the city, behold, a widow was there gathering sticks; and he called to her and said, "Bring me a little water in a vessel, that I may drink." 11And as she was going to bring it, he called to her and said, "Bring me a morsel of bread in your hand." 12And she said, "As the Lord your God lives, I have nothing baked, only a handful of meal in a jar, and a little oil in a cruse; and now, I am gathering a couple of sticks, that I may go in and prepare it for myself and my son, that we may eat it, and die." 13And Eli'jah said to her, "Fear not; go and do as you have said; but first make me a*

little cake of it and bring it to me, and afterward make for yourself and your son. ¹⁴For thus says the Lord the God of Israel, 'The jar of meal shall not be spent, and the cruse of oil shall not fail, until the day that the Lord sends rain upon the earth." ¹⁵And she went and did as Eli'jah said; and she, and he, and her household ate for many days. ¹⁶The jar of meal was not spent, neither did the cruse of oil fail, according to the word of the Lord which he spoke by Eli'jah.

He tells the widow, who God already prepared to feed him, what God said would happen, and it happened. This is what we are to do: say what God says to say, let people know what God said He is going to do.

(Luke 4:24-30) *And he said, "Truly, I say to you, no prophet is acceptable in his own country. ²⁵But in truth, I tell you, there were many widows in Israel in the days of Eli'jah, when the heaven was shut up three years and six months, when there came a great famine over all the land; ²⁶and Eli'jah was sent to none of them but only to Zar'ephath, in the land of Sidon, to a woman who was a widow. ²⁷And there were many lepers in Israel in the time of the prophet Eli'sha; and none of them was cleansed, but only Na'aman the Syrian." ²⁸When they heard this, all in the synagogue were filled with wrath. ²⁹And they rose up and put him out of the city, and led him to the brow of the hill on which their city was built, that they might throw him down headlong. ³⁰But passing through the midst of them he went away.*

Now Jesus said this in their Synagogues. Are you willing to say what God says to say in your church or fellowship? Most would not say this from a pulpit because they love the praise of men more than the praise of God. So, the widow and Naaman were blessed by God and not any one from Israel. Maybe God wants you to bless someone not in your religion or church, but you're helping someone God does not want helped. You might want to throw me off a cliff like they wanted to do to Jesus for saying this, but it is true. If you're not hearing from God to give where God says give and how much or what to give, you can't obey and you're not laying up treasures in heaven. You need to bless who God says to bless not who you want to bless or who you are told by your leaders to bless. Ask God where to give or who to help.

I would like to say here, the man of God should have been feeding the widow, not the widow, feeding him. Can you see God trying to teach him that God's ways are not Elijah's ways of doing things? He is being fed by a Gentile, remember that. Would it humble you to be fed by a widow and stay with her in her house? God is working through a gentile to sustain him. Up ahead, he is going to say I am the only one, but as you see, the birds and a widow obeyed God. God can get birds, gentile widows, rocks and so on to obey Him. Is God getting you to obey Him?

¹⁷After this, the son of the woman, the mistress of the house, became ill; and his illness was so severe that there was no breath left in him. ¹⁸And she said to Eli'jah, "What have you against me, O man of God? You have come to me to bring my sin to remembrance, and to cause the death of my son!" ¹⁹And he said to her, "Give me your son." And he took him from her bosom, and carried him up into the upper chamber, where he lodged, and laid him upon his own bed. ²⁰And he cried to the Lord, "O Lord my God, hast thou brought calamity even upon the widow with whom I sojourn, by slaying her son?" ²¹Then he stretched himself upon the child three times, and cried to the Lord, "O Lord my God, let this child's soul come into him again." ²²And the Lord hearkened to the voice of Eli'jah; and the soul of the child came into him again, and he revived. ²³*And Eli'jah took the child, and brought him down from the upper chamber into the house, and delivered him to his mother; and Eli'jah said, "See, your son lives."* ²⁴*And the woman said to Eli'jah, "Now I know that you are a man of God, and that the word of the Lord in your mouth is truth* (1 Kings 17:17-24 ESV).

Her son dies, and she accuses Elijah of causing his death. Wait, a minute. When Elijah got there, she was going to eat and then die. Elijah told her, "The jar of meal shall not be spent, and the cruse of oil shall not fail, until the day that the Lord sends rain upon the earth." They lived by the hand of God but quickly forgot. Elijah accuses God of causing the boy's death, total disrespect and pridefulness. He prays for the boy and God lets his life come back. The death was a test for Elijah, and he failed by the way he handled the situation.

The woman said to Elijah, "Now I know you are a man of God, and that the word of the Lord in your mouth is truth." It does not say he gave God the glory for the boy's life coming back into him. I wonder if he did. Let me ask a question; Are you giving God the glory before people when God uses you? The woman is like most today when you talk about Elijah; he is exalted because of signs and wonders. I wonder how many have exalted Balaam's ass? God used the ass, but when he was done using him, he was still just an ass. Just because the boy was revived does not mean Elijah obeyed God. Same as when Moses hit the rock instead of speaking to it like God told him to, it still produced water. Again, manifestation does not confirm a man's obedience, but it confirms what God wants done or allows to be done.

I was in a service where the man ministering for three nights was a gay person. When he finished ministering, I was going to rebuke him and the Apostle of that church. Some things he said about the people of that church were wrong. God told me to hold my peace. God did use him some.

I ask God, "How can you use someone like that?" He asked me, "When I wanted to speak to Balaam, what did I use?" I said, "You used an ass." Then God said, "When I finish using the ass, what was he?" I said, "He was still an ass." Then God responded, "That apostle put him in the pulpit, and he was all I had to use, but my using him didn't change him. The rock was still a rock after water came from it."

Most Christians follow a minister because of signs and wonders, wonderful personalities, and their ability to entertain. They should ask God if what the minister is saying is the truth instead of following and believing everything the minister is saying. It used to be that when correction was brought in church, most people would get convicted, but now most get offended. (Proverbs 29:18) *Where there is no prophecy the people cast off restraint".*

(Jeremiah 23:21-22) *I did not send the prophets yet the ran; I did not speak to them yet they prophesied. ²²But if they had stood in my counsel, then they would have proclaimed my words to my people, and they would have turned them from their evil ways and from the evil of their doings.*

But you see today this is what's happening in most churches; what God is telling the ministers to say is not being said. The ministers are not bringing words of correction because people get offended and will leave their church. Without correction from God, the people are casting off restraint. They think everything is fine, but it is not.

If your parents love you, they will bring correction. If your pastor loves you and doesn't bring correction, he/she doesn't love you. (Hebrews 12:6) *For the Lord disciplines him whom he loves, and chastises every son whom he receives.* The biblical definition of chastise is the act of scolding or punishing someone; to set or keep right or to make pure.

In 1 Corinthians 14:29, it says *"when we come together, let the prophets speak two or three and judge what is being said."*

If you study what the Spirit is saying in this chapter, Paul is saying; if there is no prophesying and judging, there will be confusion. That is not being done in most churches, but they teach the saints to praise and dance but not prophesy or pray for those God sends in church to be prayed for. When I say most churches, I am being hopeful some are but I do not know of one. I ask God one day, "you say your house should be a house of prayer for all people. What does that mean?" He said to me, "When you used to supervise at Burger King and Hardees, who did you cook hamburgers for?" I said whoever came in the door. He said, "That is what my house of prayer should be for, whoever comes in that door."

Jesus Cleanses the Temple

¹⁵And they came to Jerusalem. And he entered the temple and began to drive out those who sold and those who bought in the temple, and he overturned the tables of the money-changers and the seats of those who sold pigeons; ¹⁶and he would not allow anyone to carry anything through the temple. ¹⁷And he taught, and said to them, "Is it not written, 'My house shall be called a house of prayer for all the nations'? But you have made it a den of robbers" (Mark 11:15-17 RSV).

In going over this writing, God told me to add this, and He witnessed to me this is happening in most churches today. They are a den of robbers. Robbing people of prayer, money, teaching and so on. They are not building up the saints for the work of the ministry.

In other words, wasting people's time and not doing what God has anointed them to do for the benefit of who God left them to be a gift to from God. In other words, the gifts to the body which are apostles, prophets, evangelists, pastors, and teachers are exalted and wanting who they were given to as a gift from God, to praise them and lift them up rather than God.

Just like Elijah was exalted by the people and they listened to what he said rather than giving God the credit for how he was anointed by God to do the things he did. Elijah's name means the power of Yah. That's what God did. He manifested his power through Elijah.

Unity in the Body of Christ

I therefore, a prisoner for the Lord, beg you to lead a life worthy of the calling to which you have been called, ²with all lowliness and meekness, with patience, forbearing one another in love, ³eager to maintain the unity of the Spirit in the bond of peace. ⁴There is one body and one Spirit, just as you were called to the one hope that belongs to your call, ⁵one Lord, one faith, one baptism, ⁶one God and Father of us all, who is above all and through all and in all. ⁷But grace was given to each of us according to the measure of Christ's gift. ⁸Therefore it is said, "When he ascended on high, he led a host of captives, and he gave gifts to men." ⁹(In saying, "He ascended," what does it mean but that he had also descended into the lower parts of the earth? ¹⁰He who descended is he who also ascended far above all the heavens, that he might fill all things.) ¹¹And his gifts were that some should be apostles, some prophets, some *evangelists, some pastors and teachers, *[12]*to equip the saints for the work of ministry, for building up the body of Christ,* [13]*until we all attain to the unity of the faith and of the knowledge of the Son of God, to mature manhood, to the measure of the stature of the fulness of Christ;* [14]*so that we may no longer be children, tossed to and fro and carried about with every wind of doctrine, by the cunning of men, by their craftiness in deceitful wiles.* [15]*Rather, speaking the truth in love, we are to grow up in every way into him who is the head, into Christ,* [16]*from whom the whole body, joined and knit together by every joint with which it is supplied, when each part is working properly, makes bodily growth and upbuilds itself in love.* (Ephesians 4:1-16 RSV)

Where there is no prophecy, the people cast off restraint. Again, God told me a couple of years ago, in the synagogues, they let Him do extraordinarily little. Then God said most churches are synagogues today they let Him do very little.

Every time I have shared the teaching God gave me on Elijah in services, God shows me more about how not to be disobedient and prideful like Elijah was when flowing in the anointing. God told me instead to only do what He says to do and say only say what He says to say. He will perform the signs and wonders to confirm His word that He tells me to say.

Twenty-five years ago, while ministering in the Dominican Republic God told me to quit laying hands on people. I told Him, "I did not understand because the word says lay hands on the sick." He told me, "Everywhere He sent His Apostles, He confirmed His word with signs and wonders." He brought back to my memory how Moses hit the rock instead of speaking to it. Suddenly, Moses became the source in their heart, instead of God being the source. He did not do it the way God said. However, the water still came. He did not glorify God, so he would not receive the things God had for him. All those he was leading would not go into the promised land. Instead, they spent forty years in the wilderness.

After God spoke to me about Moses, I was afraid of doing the same thing. I told God I do not want a personal anointing. Take it away from me. I only want to say and do what you say. You can see Moses had the gift to hit rocks like all the other signs God put at Moses's hand to perform before the Pharaoh. When God said speak to the rock, he disobeyed.

Why didn't God stop the water till Moses did it the way God said to do it?

One service in the Dominican Republic, when they asked me to come up and minister. As I was walking up to the pulpit God said,

"Do not say a word until I tell you to speak. If they close the service and I have not told you to speak, do not even speak in the car when you leave here." Thirty minutes went by. The pastor and my interpreter brought a man to me who had a stroke outside. They wanted me to pray for him. I shook my head no, so they laid him on the altar.

Ten minutes later, God said "You can speak now." I asked the people, "Is this God's house." They said, "Yes." I ask, "Could anyone one tell me since you have been in God's house today if you have done anything God told you to do?" Everyone got quiet. I taught when we come into God's house, we need to do what He says, not what we want to do or have our program. The man lying on the altar who had the stroke came to my interpreter and wanted to say something. So, I let him. He said, "When they laid me on the altar, I knew I was going to die. When this man started talking, Jesus stood in front of me.

He walked up to me, touched me, then healed me." This is what God told me, "If I would obey Him, by saying and doing what He tells me or shows me, He would confirm His word with signs and wonders." Who got the glory when the man testified? That is correct, God. The way you have always done things can keep you back from following what God wants you to come into or advance to.

I was confident I heard from God. I felt like the Apostles when they had a few fish and loaves of bread. God told them to split amongst them what was in their hands, walk toward people sitting in groups of fifty, and feed them from their two little hands full of food.

I did what He told me to do and just like the food multiplied to feed the five thousand, God did what He told me He was going to do. He confirmed His word with a sign and wonder. I have been doing what He said for over twenty-five years. I just thought of this , how many pastors would put someone in the pulpit and let forty minutes go by and not do something about the minister not saying any thing for 40 minutes.

Try to imagine how Jesus must have thought and felt after all He did for people that the Father told Him, showed Him, and anointed Him to do. His Father (God) says, "Stop doing all that and let them crucify you." What if he told you today to walk away from all you're doing and just build up the saints for the work of the ministry?

So many ministers today are flowing in their gifts but not saying what God says. They are hitting and touching and pushing instead of going to the next level with God. That is to build up the saints for what God has anointed them to do for God. Ask God, is it time for you to go to the next level? Die to yourself for others?

This just came to me; it is like a high school person playing sports and being number one in his senior year on the team. He fails that year on purpose to stay on the team. He would rather get the recognition as number one on the team than move on up in life. He likes the personal glory. Maybe he was destined to be a coach to teach others. A lot of ministers are that way. They want all the recognition and will not build up {coach the saints} to flow with the Spirit and the gifts as they do. These ministers will end up like Moses. He lost the promises of God because he did not glorify God by obeying Him; he acted like he was the source.

Every tree that bears fruit starts over every year, bare and fruitless but pruned. Then the sun [Son] and the rain [Spirit] cause it to produce even better than last year. The pruner [God] gets the glory. They realize if it were not for the pruning, they would not produce what they are producing, along with the Son and Spirit.

Think of it this way, God is the ground, Jesus the sun and the Holy Spirit the rain. If you're planted in the ground, the sun and rain help will cause you to grow. What is in you will spring forth by them.

The sun with no rain will dry you up and destroy you; the rain without the sun will rot you. If you are not planted in the ground, the sun and rain will destroy you. You see, if you're in God you have to have the Word and the Spirit.

Who also hath made us able ministers of the New Testament; not of the letter, but of the spirit: for the letter killeth, but the Spirit giveth life (2 Corinthians 3:6 KJV).

Can you imagine doing nothing for three years. Having birds and a Gentile widow sustain you because they were being used by God to feed and shelter you? I believe you would be humble and thankful beyond what you could imagine. You would realize God is your source, not yourself. It would be a pride killer.

(Matthew 7:21-23 ESV) *"Not everyone who says to me, 'Lord, Lord,' shall enter the kingdom of heaven, but he who does the will of my Father who is in heaven. ²²On that day many will say to me, 'Lord, Lord, did we not prophesy in your name, and cast out demons in your name, and do many mighty works in your name?' ²³And then will I declare to them, 'I never knew you; depart from me, you evildoers.'*

Many teach once saved always saved. They do not know the meaning of the word saved as compared to redeemed.

(John 1:12 RSV) *But to all who received him, who believed in his name, he gave power to become children of God.*

Gave *"power to become"* does not say you **are** a child of God.

For those who are King James only:

(John 1:12 KJV) *But as many as received him, to them gave he power to become the sons of God, even to them that believe on his name.*

Again, gave "power to become" does not say you are a son.

(Romans 10:10 RSV) *For man believes with his heart and so is justified, and he confesses with his lips and so is saved.*

Justified and saved are two different words, study their meaning.

(Romans 10:10 KJV) *For with the heart man believeth unto righteousness; and with the mouth confession is made unto salvation.*

If you study what justified, and righteousness

means then compare it to saved or salvation, you will get a true meaning of the scriptures and what they mean instead of believing some denominations doctrine.

(Matthew 7:21-23 RSV) *"Not everyone who says to me, 'Lord, Lord,' shall enter the kingdom of heaven, but he who does the will of my Father who is in heaven. ²² On that day many will say to me, 'Lord, Lord, did we not prophesy in your name, and cast out demons in your name, and do many mighty works in your name?' ²³ And then will I declare to them, 'I never knew you; depart from me, you evildoers.'*

(John 17:1-3) *When Jesus had spoken these words, he lifted up his eyes to heaven and said, "Father, the hour has come; glorify thy Son that the Son may glorify thee, ² since thou hast given him power over all flesh, to give eternal life to all whom thou hast given him. ³ And this is eternal life, that they know thee the only true God, and Jesus Christ whom thou hast sent*

(Jeremiah 22:16) He judged the cause of the poor and needy; then it was well. Is not this to know me? says the LORD.

(John 10:14-15) I am the good shepherd; I know my own and my own know me, ¹⁵ as the Father knows me and I know the Father; and I lay down my life for the sheep.

(John 6:40) For this is the will of my Father, that every one who sees the Son and believes in him should have eternal life; and I will raise him up at the last day."

If you believe in Him, you will obey what He says to do by the Holy spirit.

(John 12:49-50) For I have not spoken on my own authority; the Father who sent me has

himself given me commandment what to say and what to speak. ⁵⁰And I know that his commandment is eternal life. What I say, therefore, I say as the Father has bidden me to say."

(John 5:24) *Truly, truly, I say to you, he who hears my word and believes him who sent me, has eternal life; he does not come into judgment, but has passed from death to life.*

(John 8:51) *Truly, truly, I say to you, if any one keeps my word, he will never see death."*

That's doer not just a hearer or believer. Faith without works is dead faith.

(John 10:17-18) *For this reason the Father loves me, because I lay down my life, that I may take it again. ¹⁸No one takes it from me, but I lay it down of my own accord. I have power to lay it down, and I have power to take it again; this charge I have received from my Father."*

Are you laying down your life and doing what the Father says to do and say all the time in all things?

(Isaiah 50:4-5) *The Lord GOD has given me the tongue of those who are taught, that I may know how to sustain with a word him that is weary. Morning by morning he wakens, he wakens my ear to hear as those who are taught. ⁵ The Lord GOD has opened my ear, and I was not rebellious, I turned not backward.*

(John 3:36) *He who believes in the Son has eternal life; he who does not obey the Son shall not see life, but the wrath of God rests upon him.*

You see it says obey the Son not just believe in the Son or just confess Jesus is Lord and you will go to heaven.

(John 10:25-30) *Jesus answered them, "I told you, and you do not believe. The works that I do in my Father's name, they bear witness to me; ²⁶but you do not believe, because you do not belong to my sheep. ²⁷My sheep hear my voice, and I know them, and they follow me; ²⁸and I give them eternal life, and they shall never perish, and no one shall snatch them out of my hand. ²⁹My Father, who has given them to me,[a] is greater than all, and no one is able to snatch them out of the Father's hand. ³⁰I and the Father are one."*

Here it says again my sheep hear my voice and follow me not just confess me. If you're not hearing His voice, it says you're not His sheep. You cannot follow if you're not hearing His voice. So quit listening to everyone else and learn to listen to Jesus and be led by the Spirit if you're his sheep.

Let us see how Elijah responds after three years of God feeding him through birds and a Gentile widow.

After many days the word of the LORD came to Eli'jah, in the third year, saying, "Go, show yourself to Ahab; and I will send rain upon the earth." (1 Kings 18:1 RSV)

The word of the Lord came to Elijah for the third time in this story. Let us pay attention to how the scripture at other times does not say the *word of the Lord came to Elijah*, but he does something on his own. *The word comes to Elijah, but* he does not obey fully what God told him.

Jesus wants us to be like He was on earth; only say what the Father says to say and only do what we see the Father do. God speaks to Elijah, in the third year, and told him to show himself to Ahab. God said He would send rain on the earth, just show himself to Ahab nothing else. But that is not what he did.

²So Eli'jah went to show himself to Ahab.

Now the famine was severe in Samar'ia. ³And Ahab called Obadi'ah, who was over the household. (Now Obadi'ah revered the LORD greatly; ⁴and when Jez'ebel cut off the prophets of the LORD, Obadi'ah took a hundred prophets and hid them by fifties in a cave, and fed them with bread and water.) (1 Kings 18:2-4 RSV)

Elijah's name means the strength of Jah [the Lord]; power of the Lord. Obadiah means serving Jah [the lord]; a servant of the Lord. Elijah was doing nothing for three years. Obadiah was putting his life on the line and feeding the one hundred prophets. Hiding and feeding them in the caves. I perceive he got the food from Ahab's supply because he was over Ahab's household.

⁵And Ahab said to Obadi'ah, "Go through the land to all the springs of water and to all the valleys; perhaps we may find grass and save the horses and mules alive and not lose some of the animals." ⁶So they divided the land between them to pass through it; Ahab went in one direction by himself, and Obadi'ah went in another direction by himself. (1 Kings 18:5-6 RSV)

You see how close to Ahab Obadiah was? I repeat, for three years or more, he fed the one hundred prophets and hid them from the king and Jezebel.

⁷And as Obadi'ah was on the way, behold, Eli'jah met him; and Obadi'ah recognized him, and fell on his face, and said, "Is it you, my lord Eli'jah?" ⁸And he answered him, "It is I. Go, tell your lord, 'Behold, Eli'jah is here.'" ⁹And he said, "Wherein have I sinned, that you would give your servant into the hand of Ahab, to kill me? (1 Kings 18:7-9 RSV)

Does not sound like he trusts Elijah. Sounds like he is afraid of Elijah even though he called him lord.

¹⁰As the Lord your God lives, there is no nation or kingdom whither my lord has not sent to seek you; and when they would say, 'He is not here,' he would take an oath of the kingdom or nation that they had not found you. ¹¹And now you say, 'Go, tell your lord, "Behold, Eli'jah is here. (1 Kings 18:10-11 RSV)

Elijah calls Ahab Obadiah's lord, showing no respect to a real servant of God. Same as today, most pastors and teachers show no respect to real prophets and apostles. They do not recognize them because they are not submitted to the Spirit of God. They are like Elijah; full of themselves, thinking they are the only ones. They are keeping Jesus out of their churches by not respecting God's leadership. Apostles and prophets have a different anointing than pastors and teachers. You can say they are like the husband in a marriage and the pastor and teacher like the wife. That is the way God explained it to me to teach it.

It is not a male or female thing. I usually teach that it is like this, when a family goes to the beach and the wife typically stands on the shore, she tells the children not to go to deep. However, the husband goes out into the deep and tells the children to come out deeper.

I will share what God told me years ago. God said, "The problem in the church is the same as in the world today. There are too many children being raised by single-parent mothers or single parent fathers." Either there is no man in the house or no woman in the house. No single parent can raise children like a husband and wife working together.

The same in his church; there are pastors and teachers, but no apostles and prophets. God will send a woman a good husband. The woman will not allow him to be the head, so he either leaves or submits to the woman. The same in the churches. God sends His apostles and prophets, but the pastors and teachers will not submit. The Apostle and prophets submit to the pastors and teachers, or just leave. Churches should have all five offices functioning in it. When they work together, the congregations get a balanced leadership. None of the five-fold ministries can develop the saints like God wants by themselves. All five need to be working together.

Like it or not, that is what God showed me twenty years ago. There are apostles today submitting to so-called bishops and not God. God said He set first apostles, then prophets, in the church. In every area around the world, God has His local leadership of apostles and prophets.

The pastors and teachers would rather have their church or denomination and not God's leadership. He never ordained pastors and teachers first. That is why there are hardly any prophets speaking when you come together.

True apostles and prophets bring correction which runs so called Christians off and pastors do not want that.

When Jesus said you must eat of my flesh and drink of my blood all those following Him left but the 12. You see they liked the signs and wonders and food, but to do Jesus's will that's something else. It is the Jezebel spirit's purpose to shut the mouths of the prophets and keep the people from hearing the true word of God from the Holy Spirit, which Jezebel herself did to Elijah because he was not obeying God. Jezebel works through your fleshly leadership in God's so-called house. Just like the wife will not submit to her husband the teachers and pastors will not submit to the Apostles and Prophets.

(1Kings 18:12-19) *"And as soon as I have gone from you, the Spirit of the Lord will carry you whither I know not; and so, when I come and tell Ahab and he cannot find you, he will kill me, although I your servant, have revered the Lord from my youth. ¹³Has it not been told my lord what I did when Jez'ebel killed the prophets of the Lord, how I hid a hundred men of the Lord's prophets by fifties in a cave, and fed them with bread and water? ¹⁴And now you say, 'Go, tell your lord, "Behold, Eli'jah is here" and he will kill me.' ¹⁵And Eli'jah said, "As the Lord of hosts lives, before whom I stand, I will surely show myself to him today." ¹⁶So Obadi'ah went to meet Ahab and told him; and Ahab went to meet Eli'jah. ¹⁷When Ahab saw Eli'jah, Ahab said to him, "Is it you, you troubler of Israel?" ¹⁸And he answered, "I have not troubled Israel; but you have, and your father's house, because you have forsaken the commandments of the Lord and followed the Ba'als. ¹⁹Now therefore send and gather all Israel to me at Mount Carmel, and the four hundred and fifty prophets of Ba'al and the four hundred prophets of Ashe'rah, who eat at Jez'ebel's table."*

Any time God repeats a statement three times in a story, it means pay attention to that statement. When you read the scripture, pay attention to the words God said to him. The *'word of the Lord'* came to him about what to do. Then pay attention to Elijah when those words are not spoken to him. He does his thing or what he wants to do. He does not wait on God's word like Jesus did but does what he wants to do. This is where with the mouth confession is made unto salvation. If he would have confessed to God by saying to God, "I do not know what to do.", asking, "What should I do?", and getting God's direction, he would have been saved from all his errors and hard times, even wanting to die because he did not open his mouth and confess. He did not confess that he did not know what to do.

Ahab was in Mt Carmel which means fruitful field [plentiful place]. Notice God's instruction just like Eli'jah went to show himself to Ahab.

Was Elijah A Disobedient Prideful Prophet?

Elijah means, power of Jah [the Lord]. Obadiah means, servant of Jah [the Lord].

Again, while Elijah was doing nothing for three years, Obadiah was putting his life on the line. He was feeding one hundred prophets and hiding them in caves, but never got caught. God used Elijah to show His strength and Obadiah to serve. Which one did a better job for God? For three years and probably more, Obadiah was being fruitful for God. Like I said, the length of the season depends on you. Again, Obadiah was close to Ahab, but for three years he put his life on the line by taking food from wherever he got it and feeding one hundred of God's prophets and never got caught. Even after he was told what Obadiah was doing, Elijah still insisted that he was the only one.

God told Moses, "Speak to the rock.", here He tells Elijah, "Show yourself." That is the only instruction he got from God, but he did not obey. Elijah became prideful and haughty because of the way he handled the anointing. Elijah was just a vessel, like the birds, the widow, the ass, you, and me. He was the only one, as far as he could see, even though God told him there were seven thousand who had not bowed to Baal. When Elijah was told this, he insisted he was the only one.

Like today, as I stated before, real apostles and prophets are not respected or recognized. Most pastors and teachers think they are the only ones. They are not opened to get to the top of the Christmas tree. They really do not know where they are, nor how badly they need to separate themselves to God to get pruned to be more fruitful.

An unpruned tree produces some fruit, but not the quality and amount as a pruned tree. The goal of pruning fruit trees is usually to maximize fruit yield. Unpruned trees produce large numbers of small fruit that may be difficult to reach when harvesting by hand. Branches can become broken by the weight of the crop. The cropping may become biennial (that is, bearing fruit only every other year).

These are pear trees unpruned that are being destroyed by not being pruned and producing poor quality fruit. They are in a church yard. That's a church behind the trees.

These are some of the fruits from these unpruned pear trees. That is what your fruit looks like if you are not separating to God in your season and getting pruned. You cannot identify these as pears by their appearance and you see how rough they appear and out of shape.

King Ahab was to gather 450 prophets of Baal and 400 prophets of the Asherah. Instead of Elijah doing what God said to do, and telling the people what God said, "Show yourself and I will send rain". He did what he wanted and challenged the four hundred fifty prophets of Baal. Wonder why the 400 prophets of Asherah were not there? You see when Ahab still allowed the 400 prophets of Asherah to continue in his house after seeing Baal prophets fail God used them to give him a false word and he and Jezebel were destroyed, and the dogs licked up her blood in the street.

God did not tell Elijah to do any of what he did. You can see *the word of the Lord* was absent. Remember Elijah spoke, "There will be no rain except at my word." Instead of him saying, God told him to show himself to Ahab and God would send the rain. He went and did much more, but not from God's direction. God would have been glorified if he would have done as God said and the prophets of Baal would still have bowed and said the Lord, He is God and would have been alive and true followers of God.

When Elijah finish with his performance of calling down fire. The bible says in 1Kings 18:39-40 *"When all the people saw it, they fell on their faces; and said, The Lord, he is God; the Lord, he is God."* Elijah told them to gather the prophets of Baal. He took them to the brook Kishon and killed all four hundred and fifty of them. It says "all the people" fell on their faces and said the Lord He is God. To me, this included the four hundred and fifty prophets. Elijah killed these brand-new converts. Four hundred and fifty prophets! "Can you imagine how they were affected by the manifestation of the power of God. I have to believe if they did all they did to get Baal to do something, they would definitely have been totally driven to serve God with their whole heart after seeing what God did.

All God told Elijah to do was to show himself and God would send rain. I believe that would have been a witness enough for them to bow and say, "The Lord He is God." To turned to God and realize how awesome He is, compared to who they served. Elijah didn't have the authority to tell the people to kill the king's prophets. They listened to him because of the fire and Elijah's reputation. The king said nothing. The same today, people are following signs and wonders and are not listening to the King of Kings!

I must repeat, Baal was their god but he did not perform. I am sure they became believers in God. It says all the people bowed and said the "Lord he is God". These men were good converts to God, for it says they all bowed and said the Lord He is God. As they were for Baal, they would have been even better for God. Good job Elijah in killing four hundred and fifty converts.

The people obeyed Elijah because of signs, wonders, and out of fear of not obeying him. The same is happening today. People are obeying ministers because they are fleshly heroes, not because of God. The king was in charge and Elijah was out of order by telling the people what to do instead of submitting to the King.

Many today will not speak to the sin in the leader because they falsely believe they are God's leaders, and you shall not touch God's anointed or do the prophets no harm, but they are not God's anointed but manipulators on their own account for their denomination or church. The ministers are gifts to God's people sent by Jesus but they do not function as gifts to the people and the people do not treat them as gifts from God. Elijah was out of order and in the flesh by killing the prophets who belonged to Ahab and bowed to God.

You see, the prophets he killed were Ahab's prophets of Baal. Remember Jezebel got Ahab to worship Baal. Later you will see when Ahab listened to his 400 prophets of Asherah, he and

Jezebel died. The word of the Lord did not come to Elijah as before. None of what he did regarding the fire or killing the prophets was of God.

David could have killed Saul who was trying to kill him, but he did not touch God's king. Learn a lesson from David; Saul was trying to kill him. David could have succeeded in killing Saul, but he would not touch God's king.

¹When Saul returned from following the Philistines, he was told, "Behold, David is in the wilderness of En-gedi." ²Then Saul took three thousand chosen men out of all Israel, and went to seek David and his men in front of the Wildgoats' Rocks. ³And he came to the sheepfolds by the way, where there was a cave; and Saul went in to relieve himself. Now David and his men were sitting in the innermost parts of the cave. ⁴And the men of David said to him, "Here is the day of which the Lord said to you, behold, I will give your enemy into your hand,

and you shall do to him as it shall seem good to you.' Then David arose and stealthily cut off the skirt of Saul's robe. ⁵And afterward David's heart smote him, because he had cut off Saul's skirt. ⁶He said to his men, "The Lord forbid that I should do this thing to my lord, the Lord's anointed, to put forth my hand against him, seeing he is the Lord's anointed." ⁷So David persuaded his men with these words, and did not permit them to attack Saul. And Saul rose up and left the cave and went upon his way. ⁸Afterward David also arose, and went out of the cave, and called after Saul, "My lord the king!" And when Saul looked behind him, David bowed with his face to the earth, and did obeisance. ⁹And David said to Saul, "Why do you listen to the words of men who say, 'Behold, David seeks your hurt'? ¹⁰Lo, this day your eyes have seen how the Lord gave you today into my hand in the cave; and some bade me kill you, but I spared you. I said, 'I will not put forth my hand against my lord;

for he is the Lord's anointed.' ¹¹See, my father, see the skirt of your robe in my hand; for by the fact that I cut off the skirt of your robe, and did not kill you, you may know and see that there is no wrong or treason in my hands. I have not sinned against you, though you hunt my life to take it. ¹²May the Lord judge between me and you, may the Lord avenge me upon you; but my hand shall not be against you. ¹³As the proverb of the ancients says, 'Out of the wicked comes forth wickedness'; but my hand shall not be against you. ¹⁴After whom has the king of Israel come out? After whom do you pursue? After a dead dog! After a flea! ¹⁵May the Lord therefore be judge, and give sentence between me and you, and see to it, and plead my cause, and deliver me from your hand." ¹⁶When David had finished speaking these words to Saul, Saul said, "Is this your voice, my son David?" And Saul lifted up his voice and wept. ¹⁷He said to David, "You are more righteous than I; for you have repaid me good, whereas I have repaid you evil. ⁱ⁸And you have declared this day how you have dealt well with me, in that you did not kill me when the Lord put me into your hands. ⁱ⁹For if a man finds his enemy, will he let him go away safe? So may the Lord reward you with good for what you have done to me this day. ²⁰And now, behold, I know that you shall surely be king, and that the kingdom of Israel shall be established in your hand. ²¹Swear to me therefore by the Lord that you will not cut off my descendants after me, and that you will not destroy my name out of my father's house." ²²And David swore this to Saul. Then Saul went home; but David and his men went up to the stronghold (1 Samuel 1-22 ESV).

God respects authority and so did David; Elijah did not. God made Ahab king. Like most churches today, the ministers do what they want in supposedly "God's house". They do not submit to the Spirit because they believe their way is God's way, just like Elijah did. They are killing the real converts by not allowing the move of God in God's house. Also, taking money from people (the rich included) but not asking God what to do with it.

Learn a lesson from David; Saul was trying to kill him. He could have killed Saul in the cave, but he would not touch God's anointed king. Elijah was out of order and in the flesh by killing the prophets who bowed to God. The word of the Lord did not come to him as before. None of what he did regarding the fire or killing the prophets was of God. Even in the New Testament, we see how James exalted Elijah; James 5 verse 17 & 18. He is still exalted even though he did not obey God.

Jesus said, "Truly I tell you, among those born of women there has not risen anyone greater than John the Baptist" (Matthew 11:11).

Think about that a minute. Jesus is exalting John above Elijah (or above all the prophets). We need to learn from their mistakes and teach it to the Joshua Generation. The purpose of the minister is to build up the saints for the work of the ministry. What did John do that was so great no ministers today try to duplicate what he did or talk about how great he was like Jesus did? He never built a building, had choir, taught dancing but he did say he was not worthy to unfasten Jesus's sandals. Sounds like John was humble toward his cousin.

Ministry means what God has anointed each person to do for Him. Most ministers are not building up the saints for the work of the ministry and are anti-Christ. They are not building up the saints for what God anointed the saints to do. God also told me the ministers who are telling the people what to believe for are also anti-Christ. I told God I did not understand. He said, "I want my people to do exceedingly and abundantly above all that they ask or think. The ministers have them focused on what they are teaching them to ask for and think. They are anti-Christ; they are going to hell."

The word Christ means the anointing God puts on an individual to fulfill God's purpose in that individual's life. Ministers are supposed to be building up the saints for the work of the ministry that God has anointed them to do for God. Not the leader's purpose for them. Not to fulfill the minister's vision of what the minister wants to accomplish with them. You will see in a few minutes how off Elijah was, and he stayed that way by not following God's direct orders. There is more evidence of his disobedience portrayed.

First, why did Ahab obey Elijah when he was the authority, the king? Kings listen to the prophets but make the final decision about what to do. The king was in charge, yet he allowed Elijah to kill his and his wife's prophets. I thought God told him to show himself to Ahab and God would send rain.

Elijah had also said no rain would come except by *his word*. Why is he doing all this? Elijah did not say he would fervently pray but said at his word it would rain. God told him to show himself and God would send rain. Maybe I am missing something here?

I believe God was going to stop the rain to get the people's attention, but instead, the people feared Elijah for stopping the rain and saying there would be no rain unless he said so. Elijah was taking the glory for stopping the rain and causing it to rain instead of glorifying God by letting the people know God had told him what to say and what was going to happen by the hand of God. Elijah never really got what God had for him because he did not give God the glory for what God used him to do. Who is getting the glory for what you are doing as directed from God?

⁴¹And Eli'jah said to Ahab, "Go up, eat and drink; for there is a sound of the rushing of rain." ⁴²So Ahab went up to eat and to drink. And Eli'jah went up to the top of Carmel; and he bowed himself down upon the earth and put his face between his knees. ⁴³And he said to his servant, "Go up now, look toward the sea." And he went up and looked, and said, "There is nothing." And he said, "Go again seven times." ⁴⁴And at the seventh time he said, "Behold, a little cloud like a man's hand is rising out of the sea." And he said, "Go up, say to Ahab, 'Prepare your chariot and go down, lest the rain stop you.'" ⁴⁵And in a little while the heavens grew black with clouds and wind, and there was a great rain. And Ahab rode and went to Jezreel.

The New Testament says *he Elijah fervently prayed. God said show yourself and I will send rain.* (1 Kings 18:41-45)

Elijah tells Ahab to go eat and drink, for there is a sound of rain. Ahab went. Elijah went to the top of Mt. Carmel. He cast himself down upon the earth and put his face between his knees. It does not say he prayed; that is an assumption. When God stopped the rain, He used Elijah to speak. But why didn't Elijah obey, for we know what God said? Elijah said, "By Elijah's word, it would rain." What Elijah did was against what God said, and it was not what God said to do.

Elijah supposedly praying and sends his servant seven times to look toward the sea. The seventh time his servant sees a cloud. Why is Elijah praying when he said, "By his word it would rain?" I hope you can see his pridefulness and disobedience. He tells his servant to tell Ahab to take off, lest the rain stop you. The rain came. God's hand was on Elijah. He ran before the chariot to Jezreel. No word of the Lord came to him to go, but he went. God anointed him to run and show off to get where he was not supposed to be. God did not tell him to be there.

The word of the Lord is missing again. I don't know what God told you, but God told me I have been bought and paid for with a price. I am not my own to do whatever I want or go where I want.

He gave me a free will to do whatever God tells me or go my own way. However, I chose to be a bondservant to count on Him for everything. Including directing me daily for all my needs; 24/7 direction from God. I will show you at the end of this book where God wanted him. How much time and travel he wasted not obeying? God's hand was on him to go where he was not supposed to go.

God told me to call one of my brothers one day and tell him, "You feel you're the only true Christian in the small town you are in." He said, "You're right." God said the reason he felt like that was because he was the only true Christian in that town. God also said, "He needed to leave that town."

He would not listen. He has gone downhill for at least the last fifteen years. Just today I ministered to him, and he was down because of what he has gone through. I mention to him what God told me to tell him years ago. He realized he should have listened to the word of the God.

The good news, God is bringing him back to walk with Him because of what he has done for God over the years. Although he has missed the fullness of what God had for him. Who knows the great things he would have done for God if only he had left when God said to leave?

Was Elijah A Disobedient Prideful Prophet?

There was another minister who had sheltered men and woman for thirty years. He also had a teen challenge program. He fed the hungry and so on. God told me to call him and tell him, dust off your feet and to get out of that town he was in. He said, "God told him that as well." He also said, "He was going to deal with some things first." I told him if he did not leave town now that he would end up in jail. He laughed, but after spending a lot of money on an attorney, he ended up in jail. Out of all the ministers and brothers he had met over the years, I was the only one who visited him in jail. God had told me to get out of that same county several years before and I left.

I perceive Elijah thought he would surely get to sit at the king's table after all the King seen happen. Instead, watch what happens; the word of the Lord was not spoken to him to be there. He was on his own. I do not perceive that Elijah realized that Faith comes from hearing;

so, does fear. He is about to receive a word in his spirit that will cause him to want to die.

Ahab was submitted to Jezebel not God even though he was God's king at that time. Like most ministers today submitted to something or one another rather than God. Ahab was one who also bowed after seeing what God did. He seen the prophets of Baal fail against God. Yet he came home and still did not put his house in order but summited to his wife and her god's.

Mt Carmel means, Fruitful Field [plentiful place]. The main three seasons in our growth with God are:

    Cherith - separation,

    Zarephath - purging

    Carmel - fruitful place

We are from the ground. God said from the beginning there will be seed time and harvest. After we had a fruitful season, we need to be separate unto God so He can purge us. Then we will bring forth bigger and better fruit than last season. The most dangerous time is when we are in our fruitful season. We keep producing but miss our season of separation and pruning by not listening to God because we have gotten up in pride and pride comes before a fall. We need to stay sensitive when it is time for separation, or our fruit becomes artificial. It has nothing in it real or able to nourish; it is phony, fleshly. Like Moses and Elijah, we still have the anointing God gave us as a gift, but we are using it to glorify oneself to be praised by people but not God. We will get no reward for what we do if it is not being directed by God. You can see Moses was fruitful and so was Elijah. When God wanted to bring them into a place to produce better fruit, they did not go where God wanted them to. They kept doing it their way. A good work is not the work of God if not directed by Him. The difference is one o and a capital G between good and God. At his word would mean to me as an Apostle, just speak it in front of Ahab and it would happen; but now he is praying?

(1Kings 19:1-8) *Ahab told Jez'ebel all that Eli'jah had done, and how he had slain all the prophets with the sword. ²Then Jez'ebel sent a messenger to Eli'jah, saying, "So may the gods do to me and more also, if I do not make your life as the life of one of them by this time tomorrow." ³Then he was afraid, and he arose and went for his life, and came to Beer-sheba, which belongs to Judah, and left his servant there. ⁴But he himself went a day's journey into the wilderness and came and sat down under a broom tree; and he asked that he might die, saying, "It is enough; now, O Lord, take away my life; for I am no better than my father." ⁵And he lay down and slept under a broom tree; and behold, an angel touched him, and said to him, "Arise and eat." ⁶And he looked, and behold, there was at his head a cake baked on hot stones and a jar of water. And he ate and drank and lay down again. ⁷And the angel of the Lord came again a second time, and touched him, and said, "Arise and eat, else the journey will be too great for you." ⁸And he arose, and ate and drank, and went in the strength of that food forty days and forty nights to Horeb[a] the mount of God.*

Beersheba means, well of oath, which belongs to Judah. He went there and left his servant. I perceive God wanted him, and us, to consider what oaths or vows we have made unto Him. He is trying to get his and our attention. Elijah was too caught up in himself. He was afraid because he received Jezebel's word in his heart. He did not have God's word in His heart to be there. Fear comes the same way faith does; by words that are not of God that you receive.

The word of the Lord is missing here. Is God's word missing from where you are? Wonder why Ahab would not turn to God? Wonder why some ministers today will not choose to wholly follow God instead of partially following God?

Now an angel comes to him and feeds him, and I believe the angel guided him to the cave to meet with God. God uses birds, a widow and now an angel. He still is not seeing what God is trying to show him. He does not recognize that he is not walking with God as God wants him to. Are you recognizing how you're walking with God?

Let's look at David just before fear came into his heart.

(1 Samuel 21:8-9) *And David said to Ahim'elech, "And have you not here a spear or a sword at hand? For I have brought neither my sword nor my weapons with me, because the king's*

business required haste." ⁹And the priest said, "The sword of Goliath the Philistine, whom you killed in the valley of Elah, behold, it is here wrapped in a cloth behind the ephod; if you will take that, take it, for there is none but that here." And David said, "There is none like that; give it to me."

So, the sword of Goliath just happens to be there? Seems like it should have been a collector's item not just sitting around. Seems like David would have wanted it for a reminder of the great moment in his life when he killed the giant. That sword just happened to be there.

When I first read this years ago, I had a thought that the sword was speaking to David when it was given to him. The sword said to David do you remember how you were walking with God when you killed my owner, took me from him and then chopped his head off with me? Then why are you counting on me a sword now instead of God? David did not get the word from the sword. Let's go on and see what happens.

David Flees to Gath - Another example of fear coming to a great man of God.

(1 Samuel 21:10-13) *And David rose and fled that day from Saul and went to A'chish the king of Gath. ⁱⁱAnd the servants of A'chish said to him, "Is not this David the king of the land? Did they not sing to one another of him in dances? 'Saul has slain his thousands, and David his ten thousand?" ¹²And David took these words to heart, and was much afraid of A'chish the king of Gath. ¹³So he changed his behavior before them, and feigned himself mad in their hands, and made marks on the doors of the gate, and let his spittle run down his beard.*

Like Elijah the results of not being where God wants you or not waiting or asking for direction from God. Word got in his heart and his behavior changed. Let's see what David does now.

(1 Samuel 21:14-15) *Then said A'chish to his servants, "Lo, you see the man is mad; why then have you brought him to me? ¹⁵Do I lack madmen, that you have brought this fellow to play the madman in my presence? Shall this fellow come into my house?"*

(1 Samuel 22:1-5) *David departed from there and escaped to the cave of Adullam;*

The word cave means to be naked before God. David knew to get before God. Do you need to go to the cave? Are you walking in fear? Let's see what happens for him as he got naked before God:

and when his brothers and all his father's house heard it, they went down there to him. ²And everyone who was in distress, and everyone who was in debt, and everyone who was discontented, gathered to him; and he became captain over them. And there were with him about four hundred men. 3And David went from there to Mizpeh of Moab; and he said to the king of Moab, "Pray let my father and my mother stay[a] with you, till I know what God will do for me." 4And he left them with the king of Moab, and they stayed with him all the time that David was in the stronghold. 5Then the prophet Gad said to David, "Do not remain in the stronghold; depart and go into the land of Judah." So, David departed and went into the forest of Hereth.

David stayed in the cave till he heard from God. Then he did what the messenger from God said to do. How do you think Elijah will handle the cave experience with God?

David acted like a madman, scratching on the door and spittle running down his mouth. He realized he had a problem and went to the cave until he heard from God. The prophet brought a word from God to him, and he obeyed. David was not walking with God like he was when he slayed Goliath and realized it. He went to the cave to get naked (humble) before God. Elijah could not see his disobedience and never got naked before God in the cave. David went looking for a sword and got Goliath's sword, and I perceived he was counting on a weapon more than God.

I perceive Goliath's sword reminded him of how he was counting on God back then instead of a sword. And how he was not counting on God as he used to. How about you? Are you counting on God? Are you counting on weapons or something else rather than wholly counting on God?

An angel took Elijah to a cave. Elijah did not listen to God or ask God for help. Remember, he wanted to die. He still did not realize he was counting on himself, not God. Even after God had taken care of him for three years. Can you see how God has taken care of you? He was not the only prophet that he continued to believe he was.

The word cave means to get naked before God. David purposely went into the cave to hear from God, and he heard. Elijah did not get naked but went in fully clothed in pride and came out fully clothed in pride. He asked to die. Later, he will say that he was the only one left, and they sought his life to take it away. He totally disobeys God and God told him he had 7,000 who had not bowed. I guess he forgot about Obadiah and the 100 in the cave.

Elijah laid down and slept under a broom tree and an angel touched him, and said to him, "Arise and eat." at his head was a cake baked on hot stones and a jar of water. And he ate and drank and lay down again. The angel of the Lord came again a second time. He ate again and went in the strength of that food for forty days and forty nights to Horeb, the mount of God. I would like to have the recipe for that cake that I could go for forty days without eating.

Horeb means, desolate or parched place. Are you there? If so, you are headed to the cave. Here, God is trying to get him to listen. He wants to die, but God wakes him up to feed him so he can go where God wants him to go. Remember how David said he was going to the cave and stayed in the stronghold till he heard from God? He went because he knew he needed to hear from God. Elijah got directed there but did not listen, though he heard God talking to him.

Elijah came out of the cave worse than when he went in; he did not get naked. (Perfect place to explain getting naked) David heard from God and obeyed. When did Adam and Eve see their nakedness? That's right, after they disobeyed God. Most Christians today do not see their nakedness when they disobey God. They cover up so others do not see their nakedness. God sees the cover up. Do you recognize where you are with God? Are you covering up? If you are careful in your fruitful season and separate unto God. When God speaks to you, you will never need a cave experience.

I want to share a story here. When I ministered in the Dominican Republic, God had me share with the people the fact I had three children. They were all under three years old. Every time they dirtied a diaper, I would put the diaper in a barrel. I had three barrels and each barrel had their names on it. I would put the date on the dirty diaper to remind me I had to clean up their mess. Then put the diaper in the barrel with their name on it. When the children got older, I was going to open their barrels. Show them the messes they made that I had to clean up.

Everywhere I shared this story, they would start laughing. Then I would ask, "Do you not think I would do this?" They would say, "No," still laughing. I would ask, "Why do you believe God does that to you?" I mean, I knew when I had children, I would have to clean up some messes. God made us and knew He would clean up behind us. Recognize your messes, go to God, and thank God for cleaning you up from your messes. Strive to do better. Do not go around with a messed-up "diaper", as it can hinder your spiritual walk. Babies do not realize that they are making messes, neither do some young Christians.

An older Christian need to be more sensitive to the leading of the Spirit. When they do things that were not the leading of the Spirit, repent, admit it and try again to stay out of the flesh. I wonder to this day if Adam and Eve would have gone to God. Confessed their disobedience and repented, instead of hiding. Maybe something different would have happened.

So many today think they are something because God uses them. We ministers are a gift to the body. Most do not act like a gift but think more of themselves than the body. As a gift to the body, they should edify the body for God.

When I ministered in the Dominican Republic, Haiti, and even at ministers' meetings, I would bend over, and my interpreter would get on my back. I would say, "I am like an ass and Jesus is on my back." Everywhere He leads me, I see Him do great things. However, most ministers think they're something because God uses them, and they stand up and pump up their chest like they are something. Jesus falls off their back and can no longer do what He could have done had they stayed humble and allowed Jesus to stay on them and achieve even more and greater signs and wonders. They could still use the gifts they have but like Elijah and Moses they will never get where God wanted them to get and are not going into what God has for them.

(Isaiah 6:1-5) *How God took Isaiah to the next level in God.*

In the year that King Uzzi'ah died, I saw the Lord sitting upon a throne, high and lifted up; and his train filled the temple. ²Above him stood the seraphim; each had six wings: with two he covered his face, and with two he covered his feet, and with two he flew. ³And one called to another and said: "Holy, holy, holy is the Lord of hosts; the whole earth is full of his glory." ⁴And the foundations of the thresholds shook at the voice of him who called, and the house was filled with smoke. ⁵And I said: "Woe is me! For I am lost; for I am a man of unclean lips, and I dwell in the midst of a people of unclean lips; for my eyes have seen the King, the Lord of hosts!"

God took Isaiah in the spirit to show him himself compared to God and realized his lips were not clean. If we do not separate from others, things, places, and denominations to God, we are going to have an experience to humble us. Do not be like Elijah. Open up to what God wants to do in you to grow you. We cannot continue to do what we want to do and say what we want to say and still experience spiritual growth. We will never get to the top of the Christmas tree where Jesus is. Elijah never went forward or progressed. He never achieved or walked with God to fulfill what God had in store for him.

Elisha started off with twice the anointing of Elijah. I believe God used this to humble Elijah, who thought he was so much. I perceive

God wanted Elijah to have more. He could not progress because he would not fully obey and do it God's way. Remember, Jesus could have come off the cross, but He obeyed. Are you on your cross, or are you doing your thing in God's name?

Another example of what I am talking about is in the book of Job, chapter 42, where Job answered the LORD. *I know you can do all things, and that no purpose of yours can be thwarted. I have said what I did not understand, things too wonderful for me, which I did not know. I had heard of you by the hearing of the ear, but now I see you, so now I despise myself and repent in dust and ashes.*

If Job was not right with God, God would not have said the following. After the Lord spoke with Job, the Lord told Eliphaz that He was angry with him and his two friends because they did not speak rightly of Him as Job did.

Then he tells the three of them to take seven bulls and seven rams and offer a burnt offering for them. "My servant Job shall pray for you. I will accept Job's prayer for you. I will not deal with them according to their folly. You have not spoken rightly of me as my servant Job has."

That is heavy for me! God said He would accept Job's prayers after their offering. Their offering of the fourteen animals was to no avail without Job's prayer. After Job prayed, he received double what he had before.

Take care less you are saying things to people that are not of God. I have heard ministers quote what the three friends in Job said, as if what they said was of God. God said that what they said was not of Him. Just because it is in the bible does not mean that what they are saying is of God. As it says in Job "They did not rightly speak of me." You end up in a cave because you are doing your thing, not God's. If you separate when you are supposed to, you will not end up in a cave or in fear. Elijah came to a cave and lodged there. Behold, the word of the Lord came to him. This is the fourth time the word came to him. The word of the Lord is missing on everything else he did since it came the first time, and God told him to go show himself to Ahab.

(1 Kings 19:9-14) *And there he came to a cave, and lodged there; and behold, the word of the Lord came to him, and he said to him, "What are you doing here, Elijah?" ¹⁰He said, "I have been very jealous for the Lord, the God of hosts; for the people of Israel have forsaken thy covenant, thrown down thy altars, and slain thy prophets with the sword; and I, even I only, am left; and they seek my life, to take it away." ¹¹And he said, "Go forth, and stand upon the mount before the Lord." And behold, the Lord passed by, and a great and strong wind rent the mountains, and broke in pieces*

the rocks before the Lord, but the Lord was not in the wind; and after the wind an earthquake, but the Lord was not in the earthquake; ¹²*and after the earthquake a fire, but the Lord was not in the fire; and after the fire, a still, small voice.* ¹³*And when Eli'jah heard it, he wrapped his face in his mantle and went out and stood at the entrance of the cave. And behold, there came a voice to him, and said, "What are you doing here, Eli'jah?"* ¹⁴*He said, "I have been very jealous for the Lord, the God of hosts; for the people of Israel have forsaken thy covenant, thrown down thy altars, and slain thy prophets with the sword; and I, even I only, am left; and they seek my life, to take it away."*

Like he is informing God as if God does not know. He is exalted in himself. God did not reply to his statement. He did not ask God anything, seeing as he had the answer to why he was there. He never talked to God about his fear and wanting to die. He never asks God what to do. Why didn't God deal with him about being so lifted up? Maybe because "You have not because you ask not". Have you asked God about where you are at or are you busy telling God you're the only one? Do not get there. Stay humble. Hear His voice and only do what He says. I am sure you know Jesus could have come off the cross any time he wanted, but He obeyed.

Jesus said in Luke 9:23-25, "And he said to all, "If any man would come after me, let him deny himself and take up his cross daily and follow me. For whoever would save his life will lose it; and whoever loses his life for my sake, he will save it. For what does it profit a man if he gains the whole world and loses or forfeits himself?".

God asked Elijah twice, and he answered the same both times. He could have said, "Why are you asking me again" or "God, you know all things. Have I done something wrong?" He never realized he disobeyed God and was full of himself. It gets worse. God asks Elijah, "What are you doing here?" He tells God he has been jealous for the Lord. He also says he is the only one left and they seek to take his life away. Wait a minute, why did he not say "I wanted to die but an angel fed me, and I journeyed here"? It does not say how he was directed there.

I believe he understood what the word "cave" meant [be made naked, to be bare]. He did not get naked before God but kept saying, "I am the only one". As I previously mentioned, he forgot about Obadiah, the one hundred in the cave, and what God said about the seven thousand. PRIDE! He also got the people to kill four hundred and fifty men that belonged to the king and now, the people want to kill him?

I repeat 1 Kings 19:10. *He said, "I have been very jealous for the Lord, the God of hosts; for the people of Israel have forsaken thy covenant, thrown down thy altars, and slain thy prophets with the sword; and I, even I only, am left; and they seek my life, to take it away."*

Where does it say they seek Elijah's life? Jezebel was the only one who said anything and what she said caused him to want to die, but Elijah's walk with God was not where Elijah would talk to God about his condition but just lied and said I am the only one. Where David waited to hear from God in the cave. That's the relationship David had with God. What is your relationship with God? God says my sheep hear my voice and another they will not follow.

God did not answer him but told him to stand on the mount before the Lord. Then the Lord manifested in a wind, an earthquake, and fire, but the Lord was not in any of them. God is showing him and us today that all the yelling, pushing, singing, dancing and so on going on in the churches, is not God's perfect will, even if there is some manifestation.

I do not know when Jesus ever did all that or gave instruction for all that goes on today. What has God told you about what should go on in His house and your house? I have never seen a service where the prophets spoke two or three and what they said was judged, which is what the word says to do in a gathering when we come together. Remember, manifestation or fear of disobeying Elijah caused the people to help Elijah kill four hundred and fifty prophets of Baal instead of asking the king, who was appointed by God, what to do.

Also, he didn't ask God what to do, and he was doing something God did not tell him to do. Same today, people are doing what the ministers including prophets are saying rather than what the King of Kings, Father God is saying. Who are you getting your directions from?

All we need to do is go where God sends us and say what God says to say. He will do what He wants done. That is what he told Moses and Elijah; just say what I say and go where I send you and I will send the water and rain. Do not show off like they did, or you will never get where God wants you to get.

God spoke in a still small voice. When Elijah heard it, he wrapped his face in his mantle and went out and stood at the entrance of the cave. A voice asked him again, "What are you doing here?" He answered as before. He was the only one. It's like he's informing God what God does not know. He is exalted in himself. God did not reply to his statement. He did not ask God anything since he had the answer for why he was there. He never talked to God about his fear and of wanting to die or ask God what to do. Why didn't God deal with him being so lifted up in himself? Maybe because he didn't ask for help.

(1Kings 19:15-19) *Then the Lord said to Elijah go to Damascus and anoint Hazael to be king of Syria *[16]*and Jehu to be king of Isreal; and Eli'sha the son of Shaphat of A'bel-meho'lah you shall anoint to be a prophet in your place. *[17]*And him who escapes from the sword of Haz'ael shall Jehu slay; and him who escapes from the sword of Jehu shall Eli'sha slay. *[18]*But I will leave seven thousand in Israel who have not bowed to Baal, and the ones whose lips have not kissed him. *[19]*So, he left the cave, found Eli'sha, the son of Shaphat, who was in the field plowing with twelve yokes of oxen. Eli'jah passed by him and put his mantle on him.*

Wait a minute! Did you see God tell him to anoint Hazael and Jehu and then to go anoint Elisha? He totally disobeyed God and never anointed the two kings. I told you it gets worse. Even though God told him why He wanted the 2 kings anointed.

I perceive Elijah did not agree with God to anoint them. Because he knew how God was going to use them to punish God's people. Now tell me he was not disobedient to God. Tell me why so many exalt Elijah as a great biblical hero?

He was totally disobedient here, like many today that God has used and is using. Maybe that is why they have not gone to the next level. I hope you can see why I call him disobedient and prideful. Twenty years after he died, Elisha sent a man to anoint one king. He prophesied to the other with tears because he saw what that king was going to do to the people.

The kings God told Elijah to anoint were not in leadership positions at that given time. I do not know why God waited twenty years to use Elisha to handle the job; ask Him and let me know what He tells you. I added this scripture for your reference:

Death of Ben-hadad. (2 Kings 8:7-15) *Now Eli'sha came to Damascus. Ben-ha'dad the king of Syria, was sick; and when it was told him, "The man of God has come here," ⁸the king said to Haz'ael, "Take a present with you and go to meet the man of God, and inquire of the Lord through him, saying, 'Shall I recover from this sickness?'" ⁹So Haz'ael went to meet him, and took a present with him, all kinds of goods of Damascus, forty camel loads. When he came and stood before him, he said, "Your son Ben-ha'dad king of Syria has sent me to you, saying, 'Shall I recover from this sickness?'" ¹⁰And Eli'sha said to him, "Go, say to him, 'You shall certainly recover'; but the Lord has shown me that he shall certainly die." ¹¹And he fixed his gaze and stared at him until he was ashamed. And the man of God wept. ¹²And Haz'ael said, "Why does my lord weep?" He answered, "Because I know the evil that you will do to the people of Israel; you will set on fire their fortresses, and you will slay their young men with the sword, and dash in pieces their little ones, and rip up their women with child." ¹³And Haz'ael said, "What is your servant, who is but a dog, that he should do this great thing?" Eli'sha answered, "The Lord has shown me that you are to be king over Syria." ¹⁴Then he departed from Eli'sha, and came to his master, who said to him, "What did Eli'sha say to you?" And he answered, "He told me that you would certainly recover." ¹⁵But on the morrow he took the coverlet and dipped it in water and spread it over his face, till he died. And Haz'ael became king in his stead.*

You can see Hazael called himself a dog and then killed Benhadad.

(2 Kings 9:1-10) *Then Eli'sha the prophet called one of the sons of the prophets and said to him, "Gird up your loins, and take this flask of oil in your hand, and go to Ramoth-gilead. ²And*

when you arrive, look there for Jehu the son of Jehosh'aphat, son of Nimshi; and go in and bid him rise from among his fellows, and lead him to an inner chamber. ³Then take the flask of oil, and pour it on his head, and say, 'Thus says the Lord, I anoint you king over Israel.' Then open the door and flee; do not tarry." ⁴So the young man, the prophet, [a] went to Ramoth-gilead. ⁵And when he came, behold, the commanders of the army were in council; and he said, "I have an errand to you, O commander." And Jehu said, "To which of us all?" And he said, "To you, O commander." ⁶So he arose, and went into the house; and the young man poured the oil on his head, saying to him, "Thus says the Lord the God of Israel, I anoint you king over the people of the Lord, over Israel. ⁷And you shall strike down the house of Ahab your master, that I may avenge on Jez'ebel the blood of my servants the prophets, and the blood of all the servants of the Lord. ⁸For the whole house of Ahab shall perish; and I will cut off from Ahab every male, bond or free, in Israel. ⁹And I will make the house of Ahab like the house of Jerobo'am the son of Nebat, and like the house of Ba'asha the son of Ahi'jah. ¹⁰And the dogs shall eat Jez'ebel in the territory of Jezreel, and none shall bury her." Then he opened the door and fled.

There is the possibility Ahab was king twenty years longer than God wanted him to be. All because Elijah did not go anoint who God told him to anoint. What is going on today is the same. The ministers are not anointing who God wants anointed to do what God wants them to do. From what I've seen, there is no impartation going on like Paul talks about below.

It may be the leaders are not open to God to have it happen. God told Elijah go anoint the kings, and he did not. Today, the ministers are so busy with their programs. They are not concerned with impartations. Just about everywhere I go God uses me to impart to others. I have talked to I don't know how many pastors about having impartation services for their people, but none of them want to have any.

(Romans 1:11-12) *For I long to see you, that I may impart to you some spiritual gift to strengthen you, ¹²that is, that we may be mutually encouraged by each other's faith, both yours and mine.*

I want to say what you do not sow (impartation is sowing), you do not reap. If you sow positive, you reap positive. If you sow negative, you reap negative.

Disobedience will cause a negative harvest. Elijah did not sow to the 2 kings and did not reap what God wanted him to reap because of disobedience. I hope you can see this godly principal.

How does a man go from being humble to disobedient, but God keeps him in leadership?

"When I found out David was king for forty years, I wondered how long Saul was king. I found out he was king for forty years also. I asked God, "Why He allowed Saul to be king for forty years?" God said, "Each man has his season and when it is over it is over." Saul became king because the people wanted a king, not God. The same today in America; people wanted a king rather than God. God told me He was going to give them Barack Obama, and he was going to do to America what Saul did to Israel. Saul tried to kill Israel's best man, David. Obama was going to get rid of any good leader in America so he could put in his cronies.

Four years later, God spoke to me. He said, "If his men would fully stand up for what is right, He will work a miracle in this election." Mitt Romney was His pick in 2008. I perceived he was God's pick in 2012, but he and others would not stand up against abortion and homosexuality. We had four more years of Obama. I don't know why God told me this, but he did. He gave the people what they wanted. I perceive that is why there are so many people following a man or a denomination. They choose to follow them instead of following God.

In January 1982, a lady I knew by the name of Lula Bell Betts called. She said God told her to come see me after many attempts to get me to go to church with her. I never heard someone say, "God said," before this, but I knew there was a change in this girl's life, so I listened to her. I told her I guess she should come over. While she was talking to me, I saw a train come on my property. It was so real I could not believe it. I thought, how can a train come on my property when there are no tracks. God spoke to me and said, "I am stopping by today for you to get on board and if you do not get on board today, I might not stop again." Lula Belle said one thing I will never forget. "If you are happy with what you are doing and have done with your life, keep doing it your way. If you are not, try Jesus."

To this day, I've tried Jesus's way, not mine. I went to church that night with her. I had cold chills all over my body. They said at the end of the service if anyone wanted prayer to come up. Lula Belle and I went up and knelt on the floor. I told God. "I do not understand what they are talking about: being born again, saved. I knew Lula Bella had changed. I told God if this Jesus thing is real, I will try it. The pastor came by and laid his hands on my head. When he did, heat went through my whole body. The next day, I knew I was different.

To make a long story short, I got filled with the Holy Spirit a week later. Instantly, God started using me. I prayed for 2 people in intensive care who were about to die. They were on life support; they both came out of the hospital. The leader of that church told me I had a call on my life as a minister.

He told me I needed to join that denomination, (church). I went to put my application in to join in the offering basket. Before I did, I heard God's voice say, "If you join them, you will be worse off than you were before in the denomination you grow up in." I believe it would not be of God for me to mention the names of the two denominations. He said, "I am going to teach you the truth, and the truth will make you free."

He told me years ago, like He told Ezekiel, "If you do not say what I tell you to say, and the people die in their sin, their blood will be on your hands." I have told many people over the years if I am wrong, please forgive me. If I am correct in what I am saying, your blood is off my hands.

As you see, the leaders of that church saw my call but would not help me mature or allow me to preach in their churches unless I joined them. It did not matter to them about my calling if I was not a member. God told me He was going to teach me and told me not to join any church. He has been teaching me for thirty-nine years. It will be forty years in January 2022.

God told me, He wanted me to be free to go where He wanted me to go, when He wanted me to go, and not to worry about my income or anything else. I really want you to see that God told me about what He wanted me to do.

The denominational ministers try to bind me to them and their religion. I ended up ministering at a church that seats one thousand people two hundred miles from where I lived. I ministered there several times. This was over eighteen years ago. God blessed every time I ministered there.

Sixteen years ago, the overseer asked me to be the state prophet over one hundred and fifty churches. I told him I would pray about it. Some time went by, and then he asked me to be the state apostle. I told him if he got rid of that denomination's name, I would join his group. He told me if I joined them, it would open me to minister in one hundred and fifty churches across the state. He had me minister at his church but would not open the churches under him unless I joined the group. Since then, about seven years ago, he stepped down from that denomination as a bishop focusing on what God has told him to focus on and walking as an apostle. He has come out of his denomination, wholly following God and is highly respected by me and others. He is doing a great job by what God has told me, not by my opinion.

Too many ministers are not saying what God says to say. They will not bring correction or direction. They are manipulating the people from the pulpits. The blood of the people will be on their hands. The prophets are accountable to warn people. Pastors would be better off with a small group saying and doing what God says to say or do. Instead of trying to become a pastor of a mega-church. Where the Holy Spirit is not allowed to direct the ministers. They give the people what they want rather than giving God control and doing what God wants. God told me most churches today only allow Him to do very little.

Again, like in the New Testament, they kicked Jesus out of the synagogues. Back then, it was as if the ministers did not want the people to get to know the fullness of Jesus. The ministers did not know Him in His fullness. They were controlling the people and exalting themselves. They knew some words in the bible. They did not let the Spirit of God teach them, nor had any idea how to allow God by the Spirit to lead and guide in a service. What a shame. I will be honest, many people I minister to when I ask, "Do you know the Lord?" The first thing they say is, "I do not go to church." Then I tell them going to church can be hazardous to their Christianity. Most of them agree. Then I can minister to them as the spirit leads me.

Elisha went after Elijah, and ministered to him. The word minister means to attend as menial or worshipper; to contribute, serve, wait on. Why do we call the present leaders in the church's ministers? The present-day ministers have the people ministering to them and exalting them. Like I stated before, they are the gift to the people; to build them up and not to control or manipulate. God told me several months ago that the biggest sin in the churches today is manipulation.

When God was ready to take Elijah up to heaven by a whirlwind, Elijah tried 3 times to get Elisha to tarry, but he would not. He had been with Elijah around ten years based on my studies.

The sons of the prophets in Bethel and Jericho knew God was going to take Elijah away that day. They told Elisha, but he was already aware of that. I believe that is why Elijah wanted Elisha to stay behind.

What really saddens me is that the churches are teaching the children to sing and dance but not to prophesy. Nor move in the gifts of the Spirit. However, you cannot teach the children what you do not know how to do or allow to be done.

Paul also says, when you come together, let the prophets speak two or three and judge what is being said. Why would he say judge it if every word the prophets say is from God? If everything the prophets were saying was correct, why would it need to be weighed or judged?

Read 1 Kings 22, where Ahab's prophets had a lying spirit in them. God approved it, you see they were not God's prophets but Ahab's.

(1Kings 22:19-23) *And Micai'ah said, "Therefore hear the word of the Lord: I saw the Lord sitting on his throne, and all the host of heaven standing beside him on his right hand and on his left; [20]and the Lord said, 'Who will entice Ahab, that he may go up and fall at Ra'moth-gil'ead?' And one said one thing, and another said another. [21]Then a spirit came forward and stood before the Lord, saying, 'I will entice him.' [22]And the Lord said to him, 'By what means?' And he said, 'I will go forth, and will be a lying spirit in the mouth of all his prophets.' And he said, 'You are to entice him, and you shall succeed; go forth and do so.' [23]Now therefore behold, the Lord has put a lying spirit in the mouth of all these your prophets'; the Lord has spoken evil concerning you."*

Whose prophets are speaking to you? Who are you listening to? Are you following the direction of God, man, or your flesh? Could they have a lying spirit in their mouth? Do you not realize they do and are lying to you?

I would like to add here, God told me recently that all the prophets in the media are saying what God is going to do. God spoke to me and said, "I want to know what my prophets are going to do". In other words, are they going to stand before me and hear what I want them to say and warn my people because where there is no prophecy the people cast off restraint?

(1 John 2:27 RSV) *but the anointing which you received from him abides in you, and you have no need that anyone should teach you; as his anointing teaches you about everything, and is true, and is no lie, just as it has taught you, abide in him.*

The bible says you all may prophecy. Of course, that would keep people in church too long. It would make God happy to build up the body (in his supposed house). If one has a song, let him sing it. During a service in the Dominican Republic, God told me three times to stop ministering. He told me He had given some new songs to the people. I asked, "Who had a new song?"

First time He stopped me five people young and old sang new songs. The second time God stopped me five more different people got new songs never sung before. The third time God stopped me four more people got new songs. Fourteen different people, young children, and older adults had new songs. The keyboard player played the music like he knew the songs.

Make love your aim. Earnestly desire the spiritual gifts, especially that you may prophesy. The Bible says he who prophesies speaks to men for their up-building, encouragement, and consolation. It also says he who prophesies edifies the church.

Paul says more than anything I want you to prophesy, so you can edify the people. I studied this word edify years ago, and it means putting one brick on top of another: in other words, brick by brick. If we keep prophesying how big can the church get and how powerful.

Why is this not being taught and practiced in what most say are God's houses or church like God wants? What is going on in the churches more than prophecy; Let's praise Him with dim lights and dance before Him, read the word and preach, collect money, lay hands-on people, get them slain in the Spirit, pray in tongues, take communion, and so on. Teach how to yield to the Holy Spirit and prophesy? Lord no! Do that somewhere else.

I have attended many services. When they finished with their program, they would not allow God to move. I have seen some ministers die at an early age because of not letting God do what God wants after the church does their thing.

I was in a service one day sitting up front on the alter with the bishop and I saw Jesus sitting in the center of the congregation and all the empty seats were filled with angels. I said to Jesus "You're going to do something great today." Jesus said, "If the bishop will let me." Jesus was not allowed to do anything that day.

Elijah Ascends to Heaven

(2 Kings 2:1-2) *Now when the Lord was about to take Eli'jah up to heaven by a whirlwind, Eli'jah and Eli'sha were on their way from Gilgal. ²And Eli'jah said to Eli'sha, "Tarry here, I pray you; for the Lord has sent me as far*

as Bethel." But Eli'sha said, "As the Lord lives, and as you yourself live, I will not leave you." So they went down to Bethel.

Elisha was with Elijah around 10 years. I wonder why he told him, not to tarry here? Elijah knew he was going to be taken up, I believe, after studying the whole story. He knew about impartation and anointing others. Could it be Elijah did not want to pass on to Elisha what God wanted him to receive?

I believe many people today are under ministers who do not want to see them progress or be led by the Spirit. The minsters are not building others up to walk in what God has called them to be. The ministers are not imparting as Paul said he wanted to do when he came to the Corinthian church. This is keeping the ministers from being all God wants them to be. They are holding those under them back and are therefore being held back themselves.

As you sow, so shall you reap. If you are not building others up, you will not be built up. That is why the Bible says to earnestly desire the gift of prophecy because you edify others when you prophesy.

(1 Corinthians 14:9) *for when you build others up you will be built up. When you plant a seed, you get the whole plant back. Plant one seed of corn and how many seeds do you get back?*

(2 Kings 2:3) *And the sons of the prophets who were in Bethel came out to Eli'sha, and said to him, "Do you know that today the Lord will take away your master from over you?" And he said, "Yes, I know it; hold your peace."*

The prophets knew and so did Elisha. I feel sure Elijah knew he was going to be taken up and that's why he wanted Elisha to stay behind three times.

Was Elijah A Disobedient Prideful Prophet?

(2 Kings 2:4-12) *Eli'jah said to him, "Eli'sha, tarry here, I pray you; for the Lord has sent me to Jericho." But he said, "As the Lord lives, and as you yourself live, I will not leave you." So, they came to Jericho. ⁵The sons of the prophets who were at Jericho drew near to Eli'sha, and said to him, "Do you know that today the Lord will take away your master from over you?" And he answered, "Yes, I know it; hold your peace." ⁶Then Eli'jah said to him, "Tarry here, I pray you; for the Lord has sent me to the Jordan." But he said, "As the Lord lives, and as you yourself live, I will not leave you." So the two of them went on. ⁷Fifty men of the sons of the prophets also went, and stood at some distance from them, as they both were standing by the Jordan. ⁸Then Eli'jah took his mantle, and rolled it up, and struck the water, and the water was parted to the one side and to the other, till the two of them could go over on dry ground. ⁹When they had crossed, Eli'jah said to Eli'sha, "Ask what I shall do for you,*

before I am taken from you." And Eli'sha said, "I pray you, let me inherit a double share[a] of your spirit." ¹⁰And he said, "You have asked a hard thing; yet, if you see me as I am being taken from you, it shall be so for you; but if you do not see me, it shall not be so."¹¹And as they still went on and talked, behold, a chariot of fire and horses of fire separated the two of them. And Eli'jah went up by a whirlwind into heaven. ¹²And Eli'sha saw it and he cried, "My father, my father! The chariots of Israel and its horsemen!" And he saw him no more.

Elisha Succeeds Elijah

(2 Kings 2:12-18) Then he took hold of his own clothes and rent them in two pieces. ¹³And he took up the mantle of Eli'jah that had fallen from him, and went back and stood on the bank of the Jordan. ¹⁴Then he took the mantle of Eli'jah that had fallen from him, and struck the water, saying, "Where is the Lord, the God

of Eli'jah?" And when he had struck the water, the water was parted to the one side and to the other; and Eli'sha went over. ⁱ⁵Now when the sons of the prophets who were at Jericho saw him over against them, they said, "The spirit of Eli'jah rests on Eli'sha." And they came to meet him and bowed to the ground before him. ¹⁶And they said to him, "Behold now, there are with your servants fifty strong men; pray, let them go, and seek your master; it may be that the Spirit of the Lord has caught him up and cast him upon some mountain or into some valley." And he said, "You shall not send." ¹⁷But when they urged him till he was ashamed, he said, "Send." They sent therefore fifty men; and for three days they sought him but did not find him. ¹⁸And they came back to him, while he tarried at Jericho, and he said to them, "Did I not say to you, do not go?"

Elijah told Elisha, "Ask what I shall do for you, before I am taken from you." Elisha said, "I want a double portion of your Spirit" or anointing as I see it. I always wondered, if Elisha asked for more than double, would he have gotten it? God said He can do exceedingly abundantly above what we ask or think. What are you asking for from God?

Elijah said, "It is a hard thing you ask, but if you see me as I am being taken up, it will happen for you." You see, Elijah knew he was going to be taken up and tried to get Elisha to stay behind three times. Why would he want Elisha to stay back? I believe Elijah didn't want to impart to Elisha. Just like many ministers today. They don't want to impart to those under them. What they don't realize is that it is in imparting to others that they receive more impartation than what they have.

A chariot of fire with horses of fire separated the two. Elijah went up by a whirlwind into heaven. This is where I believe God dealt with

Elijah's pride by giving Elisha twice the anointing he had. He could have had at least twice the anointing than what he had. All he had to do was be humble, get rid of his pride or confidence in himself more than God, and obey God's voice.

All this is in the bible. When this next move of the spirit comes, we can learn from these stories and will not mess up. God can keep giving us more anointing because we are being faithful over what He has already given us to use if we are being directed by His Spirit fully; not partially, but fully.

You must stay humble if you are going into the promise land that is coming in the spirit. God told me thirty-nine years ago that He called me to be a Joshua. He was going to use me to help take the next generation into the promise land. The last generation He set free. They did not want to wholly follow God. Instead, they became religious, did their thing, not God's thing, even in the house of God. They became synagogues run by the people. Not God's temples, where God moved like he wanted to. Joshua and Caleb are the only Two who wholly followed God. That does not mean Moses, and the others did not follow God; they did at times, but not wholly. The same today, many have not sold out to eat His meat (food) and drink His blood.

I believe God wants me to share a testimony. Around twenty-five years ago, I went to Columbia S.C. to minister to a family. I ended up ministering for thirty nights straight in five churches. There are many stories I can tell, but there is one I need to tell.

I started sharing at two different churches. Two angels were at the back doors waved at me and said, "Hi Andy, we are going to touch anyone you send to the back doors." I repeated what they said. Every person God sent to the back door in some form, or another was touched by the angels. God did this for five days straight in both churches.

One night there were about eight to ten people hanging around after service. Everyone else had left. God said, "Tell them to get in the center aisle, stand behind each other, and to raise their hands." As I told them, I saw angels standing on the right and left of each person.

When they raised their hands, the angels touched their hands. They all fell backward at one time landing on top of one another. God got the glory, not me. I told them what God said for them to do. Then God did what God wanted to do. Just because you have an authority does not mean you should do what you want without direction from God. The simplest way to explain this is we have been bought and paid for and we are not our own. When we get our paycheck, we can do whatever we want with it, or we can obey God's direct direction on what to do with what belongs to God, which is all of it. We are not our own, neither anything we have.

That is how it is with the spiritual things He puts in your hands to use for His glory. He gives you control; they belong to Him, but you can use them as you want or as He directs you. You can do what you want or be led by Him, your choice.

To sum it up, God put this story in the bible so we could learn from Elijah and Elisha's walk with God. What to do and what not to do. Please ask God to help you fully follow Him day and night. To separate from whom God says separate, to go where God says to go, including Church or fellowship. Bad company ruins good morals. Do not keep company with fleshly led Christians if you are led by the Spirit of God. You cannot choose who to minister to or help, but you can choose who to hang with.

Was Elijah A Disobedient Prideful Prophet?

I was accused in Tennessee by a Pastor and some of the people of being a lone ranger. They had a conference and invited me to be there. One of the leaders in the church stood up and said God just spoke to me about Andy. Me and the pastor were agreeing Andy was a loner but God just spoke to me and said Andy is walking with Jesus and is not alone.

(John 6:52-66) *The Jews then disputed among themselves, saying, "How can this man give us his flesh to eat?"[d]* *53So Jesus said to them, "Truly, truly, I say to you, unless you eat the flesh of the Son of man and drink his blood, you have no life in you; 54he who eats my flesh and drinks my blood has eternal life, and I will raise him up at the last day. 55For my flesh is food indeed, and my blood is drink indeed. 56He who eats my flesh and drinks my blood abides in me, and I in him. 57As the living Father sent me, and I live because of the Father, so he who eats me will live because of me.*

⁵⁸ This is the bread which came down from heaven, not such as the fathers ate and died; he who eats this bread will live forever." ⁵⁹This he said in the synagogue, as he taught at Caper'na-um. ⁶⁰Many of his disciples, when they heard it, said, "This is a hard saying; who can listen to it?" ⁶¹ But Jesus, knowing in himself that his disciples murmured at it, said to them, "Do you take offense at this? ⁶²Then what if you were to see the Son of man ascending where he was before? [e] ⁶³It is the spirit that gives life, the flesh is of no avail; the words that I have spoken to you are spirit and life. ⁶⁴ But there are some of you that do not believe." For Jesus knew from the first who those were that did not believe, and who it was that should betray him. ⁶⁵And he said, "This is why I told you that no one can come to me unless it is granted him by the Father." ⁶⁶After this, many of his disciples drew back, and no longer went about with him.

Many today when God tells them it is time to eat my meat (food) and get off the milk that is for babies, draw back and do not obey any further. They like playing church but do not want to follow the Holy Spirit and serve or eat meat. It is more fun to baby everyone. In other words keep them on the milk instead feed them meat. This scripture always reminds me of Jesus at the well with a Samaritan woman who the Jews did not talk to.

God just told me to share 1 Cor. 2:1-5: *When I came to you, brethren, I did not come proclaiming to you the testimony[a] of God in lofty words or wisdom. ² For I decided to know nothing among you except Jesus Christ and him crucified. ³And I was with you in weakness and in much fear and trembling; ⁴and my speech and my message were not in plausible words of wisdom, but in demonstration of the Spirit and of power, ⁵that your faith might not rest in the wisdom of men but in the power of God.*

On Divisions in the Corinthian Church

Then 1 Corinthians 3:1-9: *But I, brethren, could not address you as spiritual men, but as men of the flesh, as babes in Christ. ²I fed you with milk, not solid food; for you were not ready for it; and even yet you are not ready, ³for you are still of the flesh. For while there is jealousy and strife among you, are you not of the flesh, and behaving like ordinary men? ⁴For when one says, "I belong to Paul," and another, "I belong to Apol'los," are you not merely men? ⁵What then is Apol'los? What is Paul? Servants through whom you believed, as the Lord assigned to each. ⁶I planted, Apol'los watered, but God gave the growth. ⁷So neither he who plants nor he who waters is anything, but only God who gives the growth. ⁸He who plants and he who waters are equal, and each shall receive his wages according to his labor. ⁹For we are God's fellow workers; you are God's field, God's building.*

Take it in what God just had me put in this letter. *⁷So neither he who plants nor he who waters is anything, but only God who gives the growth.* Quit lifting up God's gift to you, the ministers. Get off the milk and start eating meat.

(Hebrews 5:5-14) *So also Christ did not exalt himself to be made a high priest, but was appointed by him who said to him,"Thou art my Son, today I have begotten thee"; ⁶as he says also in another place, "Thou art a priest for ever, after the order of Melchiz'edek." ⁷In the days of his flesh, Jesus[a] offered up prayers and supplications, with loud cries and tears, to him who was able to save him from death, and he was heard for his godly fear. ⁸Although he was a Son, he learned obedience through what he suffered; ⁹and being made perfect he became the source of eternal salvation to all who obey him, ¹⁰being designated by God a high priest after the order of Melchiz'edek.*

Warning against Falling Away

¹¹ *About this we have much to say which is hard to explain, since you have become dull of hearing.* ¹²*For though by this time you ought to be teachers, you need some one to teach you again the first principles of God's word. You need milk, not solid food;* ¹³*for every one who lives on milk is unskilled in the word of righteousness, for he is a child.* ¹⁴*But solid food is for the mature, for those who have their faculties trained by practice to distinguish good from evil.*

You see the ministers are keeping you on milk if you can see that. God wants you to eat his meat.

(John 4:4-9) *He had to pass through Samar'ia.* ⁵*So he came to a city of Samar'ia, called Sy'char, near the field that Jacob gave to his son Joseph.* ⁶*Jacob's well was there, and* so Jesus, wearied as he was with his journey, sat down beside the well. It was about the sixth hour. ⁷There came a woman of Samar'ia to draw water. Jesus said to her, "Give me a drink." ⁸For his disciples had gone away into the city to buy food. ⁹The Samaritan woman said to him, "How is it that you, a Jew, ask a drink of me, a woman of Samar'ia?" For Jews have no dealings with Samaritans.

(John 4:27-34) *Just then, his disciples came. They marveled that he was talking with a woman, but none said, "What do you wish?" or, "Why are you talking with her?" ²⁸So the woman left her water jar, and went away into the city, and said to the people, ²⁹ "Come, see a man who told me all that I ever did. Can this be the Christ?" ³⁰They went out of the city and were coming to him. ³¹Meanwhile the disciples besought him, saying, "Rabbi, eat." ³²But he said to them, "I have food to eat of which you do not know." ³³So the disciples said to one another, "Has anyone brought him food?" ³⁴Jesus said to them, "My food is to do the will of him who sent me, and to accomplish his work.*

He broke the Jewish rules of interacting with a Samaritan, especially a woman. He obeyed the Father. Are you going by rules of men or your religion or obeying God?

I want to share a brief story about a guy I know who was fifty years old when God told him a twenty-two-year-old black girl was going to be his wife. He fought with God for two years. He thought he lost his marbles. In fact, he told God if he was going to hell, he would still serve Him because God deserved that. She was twenty-eight years younger than him. He was white.

God showed her as well. She turned down a singing career with Gloria Gaither's son. The two got married two years later. He was fifty-two, and she was twenty-four. He said he was not going to have any children.

A minister friend of his wanted the man to buy his bus. The man had no use for the bus. A few weeks later, while attending a church service, a woman told him that God said to give him $100. He knew it was for the bus he did not want.

The apostle of that church, who was a friend of the man, took up an offering and gave him the money for the bus. He tried to get a minister in Tennessee to figure out where to donate it. Long story short, it was going to go to an orphanage in Sonora, Mexico. They loaded it to the top with all kinds of stuff. The people who were supposed to take it could not go, so the man and his wife were told by God to take it. All the way there over two days, he kept asking God, "Why do you have us doing this?" They delivered the bus to the orphanage. The man running the orphanage was forty-eight years old and taking care of seventy-five children by himself. His wife had left him.

When my friend heard this, God spoke to him and said, "This man is willing to take care of seventy-five children for me. What's your problem?" He had been doing a lot of ministries oversees and thought he was too busy and too old to have children.

The man got humbled. They now have nine children; his fifth born on his 62th birthday and the last one born when he was seventy. God told them to give up their visions for His; it is called dying to self (or drinking God's cup).

In the year 2021, their youngest is seven, and the oldest is twenty-three; the man is seventy-seven. They got married on Friday November 22, 1996. The first child was a boy. God said,

"Name him Samuel. He will be a prophet." He was born on Friday August 22, 1997, nine months later.

A few months after Samuel was born, when ministering In Haiti, the man showed the ministers the baby's picture. They ask, "What is his name?" The man told them to ask God. The did, God told them, "His name is Samuel. He will be a prophet."

If you haven't figured it out, I am that man. You see, my children are covenant children with God because He ordained them. I did not choose her, nor did she choose me. God said for us to get married. God put us together. What God put together, let no man put asunder. Look at the trouble God went through to get Ruth to Boaz, a Moabite in the lineage of Jesus.

Name of places and their meanings where Elijah walked.

Gilead - heap of testimony, witness.

Jordan - a descent, literally to go downward.

Cherith - separation from something to God.

Zarephath - refinement [purge away].

Carmel - fruitful field [plentiful place].

Beersheba - well of oath.

Horeb - desolate, parched.

Cave - be made naked [to be bare].

The distance in miles Elijah went.

Gilead to Cherith	30 miles
Cherith to Zarephath	75 miles
Zarephath to Carmel	52 miles
Carmel to Jezreel	25 miles
Jezreel to Beersheba	98 miles
Beersheba to Horeb	200 miles
Horeb to Damascus	420 miles
	Total 900 miles

The distance in miles the way God planned.

Gilead to Cherith   30 miles

Cherith to Zarephath   75 miles

Zarephath to Carmel   52 miles

Carmel to Damascus   92 miles

Total   249 miles

Elijah would have saved 651 miles if he had waited for the *Word of the Lord* for direction at Mt Carmel instead of going to Jezreel. It took him forty days to travel from Beersheba to Horeb. Which is an average of five miles a day travel, so 651 miles would be approximately 130 days of travel. 450 men would still be alive, serving God. He would not have wanted to die. And so much more. Please pray for yourself to open up and be taught by the Holy Spirit.

Meaning of some names.

Ahab - brother [friend of his father]

Elijah - strength of Jah [the Lord]

Elisha - God is salvation

Obadiah - serving or servant of Jah [the Lord

Tishbite - recourse

Shaphat - judge

Abelmeholah - meadow of dancing

Jezebel - chaste, unexalted new testament– false teacher, or violent, shrewish woman.

Kishon Snarer, Place Of The Snaring

Apostle Andrew Giannelli

A messenger of God

**CONTACT INFORMATION FOR
APOSTLE ANDREW GIANNELLI
Email:odm@homesc.com**

Apostle Andy and Family

www.ingramcontent.com/pod-product-compliance
Lightning Source LLC
Chambersburg PA
CBHW072012070526
44583CB00015B/1441